W9-BXW-081

Campus Voices and Student Choices

Presented to:

____

From:

____

Date:

____

Campus Voices and Student Choices

A Daily Devotional and Daily Journal for College Students

Reflections and Advice from Interviews with Freshmen, Upperclassmen, Graduates, and Administrators

A Valuable Resource for Surviving the Transition from High School to College

---

D. Tony and Kathy M. Willis

Copyright © 2009 by D. Tony and Kathy M. Willis

Campus Voices and Student Choices
A Daily Devotional and Daily Journal for College Students
Reflections and Advice from Interviews with Freshmen, Upperclassmen, Graduates, and Administrators
A Valuable Resource for Surviving the Transition from High School to College
by D. Tony and Kathy M. Willis

Printed in the United States of America

ISBN 978-1-60791-680-2

All rights reserved solely by the author. The author guarantees all contents are original and do not infringe upon the legal rights of any other person or work. No part of this book may be reproduced in any form without the permission of the author. The views expressed in this book are not necessarily those of the publisher.

Unless otherwise indicated, Bible quotations are taken from The Kings James Version.

www.xulonpress.com

DEDICATION

We lovingly dedicate this book to Stephanie and Jonathan. You have made us so proud to be your parents. We pray that God will not only bless and keep you as students, but that He will also bless and keep you throughout your lives.

And we dedicate this book to other students who have chosen to attend an institution of higher learning as a step in pursuing their destiny.

TABLE OF CONTENTS

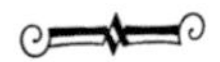

PREFACE

Transition. This word reminds us of the times we have faced the challenge of making a change. Life throws many such opportunities our way. They often bring with them a great deal of fear and anxiety.

In childhood, a youngster must adjust to leaving the security of home and entering kindergarten, a move that will likely cause tears. Each new school year brings the necessity to adapt, to make new friends. The same adjustment occurs when parents move a child to another school district or to a new church. A young adult may get a job, where he must learn the ropes and get to know other employees. Moving away from home to an apartment represents yet another change, as does repeating vows to get married.

The transition from high school to college stands as one of the most difficult transitions for young people. Just as a child may have cried upon entering kindergarten, he or she may well cry upon entering college. We wrote *Campus Voices and Student Choices* primarily to help freshmen deal with the alarm they may feel, as well as to help upperclassmen focus on the goal of finishing school. The latter will find the last few chapters, in particular, of help in achieving their goal of graduation.

Campus Voices and Student Choices will give you a daily source of spiritual strength to help guide you through this transition with a daily devotional for every day of a semester (16 weeks/112 days). Each brief devotional requires no more than five minutes to read. Each weekly chapter introduction begins with a list of the devotional topics for the week and, in a segment titled "Voices and Choices," provides relevant quotes from students, graduates, and administrators. Each chapter introduction concludes with a journal focus thought and a special prayer for the week.

Each daily devotional contains three important elements. First, the devotional begins with a scriptural insight, using the King James Version of the Bible. You may also wish to look up the daily scriptural insight verses in the biblical translation that you prefer. Second, each day has a special devotional focus. This section gives some relevant stories, comments from other students, or thought-provoking insights. Third, the daily devotional concludes with a journal reflection. Here, you may express how college is impacting your life. Writing often helps a person to clarify feelings and to find direction.

We graduated from college 25 years ago. How we wish that we had written down what we experienced during our life-changing collegiate journey. We strongly encourage you to keep a journal. In the years ahead, you will be glad that you did. Your journal reflection will one day remind you of the many ways that the Lord sustained you during this demanding time.

Influence. This word reminds us of people to whom we look for advice and direction. As role models, they help shape us, affect our decisions, and determine our future. What we see and read will also influence us. We hope that *Campus Voices and Student Choices* will have an invaluable influence upon you, not only during your college years, but also throughout your life.

We know that many of you will never struggle with some of the issues that are presented in these devotions. We hope that this book will equip you to positively influence others that may be struggling with some of the issues that have been addressed.

A few people have remarked that this book may be too religious for students. As we considered their observations, we thought of a recent study. It found that about half of the young people who entered college as Christians left college denying their faith. We understand that about 1,700 college students die from alcohol-related accidents each year. Many who grew up in church quit attending a house of God once they were on their own and free to make their own decisions. We, personally, know a number of students who have returned from college with terrible hurts and deep wounds as a result of disastrous decisions they made.

With so many voices swaying students negatively, we feel a strong voice is needed to influence students positively. We have confidence that Christian college students want someone to disciple them, challenge them, and help them deal with the many difficult situations they may face in a strong and straightforward manner.

We pray that this book will strengthen, encourage, and instruct you during your collegiate journey.

ACKNOWLEDGMENTS

We would first like to acknowledge that the Lord inspired and enabled us to write this book. He answered our prayers for strength and insight as we attempted to give this book our very best.

Our children, Stephanie and Jonathan, gave us special insight into the many issues that we needed to address in this book. We thank you for being open about the student experiences that have caused you to struggle. We have written this book to help you. Thank you to our families for your love and prayers and for bringing us up as Christians.

We thank Lee University for an education that has opened many doors and prepared us to walk through them and Gary Ray for sharing the Frontline information with us.

We offer special thanks to Dr. Paul Conn for sharing some of his feelings and experiences of being a freshman. Your thoughts inspired us to help students going through the trauma of transition. Your love, vision, and the many sacrifices you have made for Lee University are greatly appreciated by your students and the alumni.

We thank the leaders of Liberty University for the tremendous spiritual influence that exists upon the Liberty University campus. We honor the memory of the late Dr. Jerry Falwell. His anointed chapel services and his love for the spiritual well-being of his students will never be forgotten.

We are especially grateful to all the students and graduates who allowed us to interview them. Your advice and the lessons you shared will certainly help other students. Thanks for taking the time to answer our questions and agreeing to be anonymous. This book would have been much larger and much more complex if we had included all your names and schools.

Thanks to Madilee C. Wnek for her expertise in proofing and editing. This was not an easy job, and we appreciate your willingness to tackle it. Words can never truly express how grateful we are. Thanks also to Patti A. Lee for her final proofing.

Thanks to Dr. Michael Baker for your creative insight and support and for the important changes that you suggested as we wrote this book.

Finally, we thank our spiritual family at Soul's Harbor for your great love and support.

INTRODUCTION

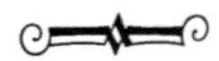

The time had finally arrived. Years of getting up early, writing papers, and taking tests had come to an end. With your cap and gown measured and your senior pictures handed out, you attended special school activities for your class. Graduation announcements sent to family and friends brought surprises and fun as gifts arrived. You signed your classmates' yearbooks as they signed yours, then read and reread their sentiments. And your class practiced for the big day. Before you knew it, family and friends had gathered for your special moment and you were walking down the aisle while the orchestra played "Pomp and Circumstance." Waiting for the diploma ceremony to begin, you listened to special guests, school administrators, and students. Finally, you heard your name echoing over the loudspeaker, and you strode forward with pride to the cheers and tears of your loved ones. At the conclusion, you joined others in throwing your hat into the air and basking in the congratulations.

After the ceremony, you showed your diploma to everyone at a special gathering to honor you, and they beamed with pride at your accomplishments. They also bombarded you with some of the same questions that you had been hearing for months:

"Are you going to continue your education?"
"Where are you going to college?"
"What do you plan to major in?"
"What are you going to do with your life?"
"What's next for you?"

You tried to answer their questions to the best of your ability, but inside you realized that you had questions of your own that needed answers. That's when reality struck you. High school and life as you had known it was over, and you felt ill prepared for the future. That night in bed you recalled the graduation ceremony and receiving your diploma, a milestone that gave you great pleasure. Yet, you also thought about your questions, and you felt afraid as you contemplated the changes ahead.

Even before graduation, some of your friends had already made life choices, opting to move directly into the work force or to join the military, even discussing marriage. Some appeared confident about their plans, while others seemed confused. With college in your future, you had likely visited the school of your choice, deciding whether to commute to school or move into a dormitory. You had taken the ACT or SAT test and filled out financial aid forms, glad for the college savings that your parents had set aside for you. But, as your summer ended, many nagging questions plagued your mind: questions about friends, roommates, money, classes, grades, and whether you would like the school you had finally chosen.

Our children, too, faced these questions, and we helped them through this process. We remember arriving at their school and seeing the trauma of transition on the faces of many students. It reminded us of the transition and excitement we felt on leaving home and moving into our college dormitories. That day we talked to many students, and we could tell that most were totally overwhelmed. Some laughed nervously and tried quickly to make friends; others withdrew from everyone and wept secretly. As we watched these freshmen endure this difficult time, my wife and I talked about the need for a book that would help freshmen and upperclassmen survive it. That's when the idea for a collegiate devotional book was born.

While this book is our first attempt at ministering to others through writing, my wife and I are experienced in helping students face this transition. Because we want to expand our reach to many others, this book became our dream.

Over the past three years, we have interviewed high school and college students, graduates, teachers, and administrators from more than 40 colleges and universities, both public and private.

Throughout this book, we use the word "college" to represent all these institutions. Those interviewed represent a broad spectrum of interests and careers, and we have promised them that they would remain anonymous.

We asked a variety of questions depending upon the person interviewed. Here is a sampling of our questions to students:

"What do you think will be your hardest challenge as you begin college?"
"What has been your hardest struggle since you started college?"
"What advice would you offer to other students?"
"What do you want other students to learn from your challenges or mistakes?"

They eagerly answered these questions and usually thanked us for taking the time to talk with them. We've included their comments on their struggles and mistakes, as well as their advice in the weekly "Voices and Choices" segment. This book addresses many important issues that every student will face.

When sharing with the students our dream of producing this book, most of them exclaimed, "Oh, we need a book like that!" Others wondered, "Why hasn't someone done that already?" Several students have told us that they often feel they are all alone in resisting those who try to drag them into the party scene. These student reflections have inspired us to name this book, *Campus Voices and Student Choices*.

We encourage you to use this book to help you make wise choices as you stand strong in your faith. May God bless you on your journey.

Campus Voices and Student Choices

Chapter One

A New Chapter Has Begun

1. *Your Future Starts Now*
2. *Looking Forward to College*
3. *Student Voices*
4. *A New Door Has Opened*
5. *Put Your Best Foot Forward*
6. *Follow Your Dream*
7. *You Better Recognize*

Voices and Choices

"I'm so excited to be on my own."

"My first semester was the hardest. I would tell freshmen that it really does get easier."

"I would tell new students to get plugged in."

"When I came to the university, I didn't want to leave my room.

"Finally, I branched out, and then I liked it."

"I didn't fit in at first."

"I was really unprepared for school."

"I was very sheltered. When I went to school, I had to learn to make my own decisions. It was like being thrown into the water and told to learn to swim."

Journal Focus

This chapter focuses upon your destiny and upon the exciting new chapter that you are beginning. As you make journal entries, write about the struggles you are encountering, your first impressions of school, and the victories you have already won.

Strength Through Prayer

"Dear Heavenly Father, facing new challenges is not easy. The events over the last few days have been hard. Please help me as I try to adjust to the new surroundings and the changes that are happening in my life. Amen."

Your Future Starts Now

Scriptural insight:

Now the Lord had said unto Abram, Get thee out of thy country, and from thy kindred, and from thy father's house, unto a land that I will shew thee: And I will make of thee a great nation, and I will bless thee, and make thy name great; and thou shalt be a blessing. (Genesis 12:1-2)

Let's begin your semester by looking at a story in the book of beginnings (Genesis). Knowing which way to go and what to do is simple when you have divine direction. So it was for Abraham. The Lord told him to leave his country and his people. Although he faced the uncertainty of the future, he had the assurance that God had given him direction. God promised to reward his obedience, telling Abraham He would make him a great nation and would make his name great.

Long before God made Abraham great, He gave him instructions. Abraham made a decision to be obedient and to trust God with his future. He also endured the painful sacrifices that, no doubt, accompanied leaving his home. He placed himself into the hands of the Lord. The future may have been a mystery to him, but he knew that God had a plan for his life.

God often requires that we move forward with faith and trust in Him. He often reveals just the first step that we should take in our journey. Like Abraham, we take the first step not knowing the particulars of God's plan.

God fulfilled all the exciting promises He had made to Abraham and rewarded his obedience and faith with extraordinary spiritual blessings. God still blesses those who trust Him and place their lives into His hands.

Devotional focus:

The valedictorian of a graduating class gave a commencement address using a phrase that may be called a cliché. The senior told his classmates, "A new chapter has begun." This is a common phrase used at many graduation ceremonies. Speakers want to emphasize that the graduates are entering an exciting new period in their lives.

This cliché makes me think of the life chapters that have already been written. The first chapter would be about birth and the early years. Family history, accomplishments, and dreams would comprise other chapters. Learning to drive and landing a job might be a part of other chapters. Then, high school years would precede the new chapter now being written.

This new chapter will be filled with many changes—perhaps a new job and a new home, a marriage, and for some a new college campus where the freshman will encounter new friends, new thoughts, and new ideas. As you write this new chapter, please fill the pages to reflect your history with good choices, decisions, and actions. Let this chapter truly be an exciting and wonderful chapter. What do you want this chapter to say?

Journal reflection:

Looking Forward to College

Scriptural insight:

Where no counsel is, the people fall: but in the multitude of counselors there is safety. (Proverbs 11:14)

Trust in the Lord with all thine heart; and lean not unto thine own understanding. In all thy ways acknowledge him, and he shall direct thy paths. (Proverbs 3:5-6)

If you ever have the opportunity to serve on a committee, you will make some interesting discoveries. You will learn that people come to the table with varying degrees of experience. You will see that wisdom can come from the young, as well as the old. You will find that you may look at an issue in many different ways, and rarely does everyone share the same viewpoint. You will see that wisdom often dictates that one may have to change his mind about an issue, as the committee members work to make the best decision and to fulfill the purpose for which they were chosen. The many voices from the committee help the group to make better decisions.

In life, many come to the table having learned from various experiences. As you prepare to face upcoming challenges, they may be able to offer just the advice you need. People around you have already survived an array of tests. They want to tell you how to survive, and they want to help as much as they can.

The Bible lets us know that we need the wisdom, counsel, and advice of those around us, without which we would certainly suffer. Solomon let us know safety lies in good counsel. Facing new challenges in college requires that we ask questions and listen to others as we look forward.

Devotional focus:

Couples approaching marriage often ask for premarital counseling. A good counselor helps them determine if they are ready for marriage, looking ahead to detect any areas where there might be problems and addressing those issues now to prevent marital problems later. Areas of concern usually include communication, finances, conflict, in-laws, religion, and family planning. Pre-marital counseling has been a great help to many couples.

If pre-college counseling were available, I wonder what the topics of discussion would be. I know that many high schools offer guidance counseling to help their students face transition during those years; however, students heading off to college have a whole new set of issues to consider:

- Expect to be asked to declare a major. Choose a major that you enjoy and anticipate graduating with a degree that you can use in your career.
- Expect to have some tears at times. Realize that your tears will dry as you adjust.
- Expect to miss your family and friends. Make a habit of calling and writing to them often.
- Expect to be lonely sometimes. Push yourself to make new friends.
- Expect to see diversity on a college campus. Learn to appreciate others.
- Expect to be tempted to hole up in your dorm room. Make yourself get involved.
- Expect to have trouble fitting in at first. Find a place where you fit.
- Expect to have to apply yourself/work if you are to be successful. Learn good work ethics that will lead to a successful life.
- Expect to be challenged and changed. Understand that being stretched is good for you.
- Expect to endure some conflict at times. Learn how to deal with difficult people.
- Expect to have some times of frustration and pressure. Discover healthy ways to let off steam.
- Expect to be extremely busy. Practice good time-management skills.
- Expect to have some failures along with your successes. Remember that failures also offer valuable lessons.

- Expect to learn to do laundry and to cook. Learn these basic necessities at home or find a friend to teach you.

Journal reflection:

Student Voices

Scriptural insight:

Through wisdom is an house builded; and by understanding it is established: and by knowledge shall the chambers be filled with all precious and pleasant riches. A wise man is strong; yea, a man of knowledge increaseth strength . . . and in multitude of counselors there is safety. (Proverbs 24:3-6)

"There is safety in numbers," goes a much-quoted saying. People often give this advice to inspire someone to seek counsel rather than brave it alone. Solomon talked about another reason to listen to advice. With their distinct experiences and backgrounds, others have a unique perspective and often see aspects of a matter that we may have missed. Occasionally, a leader will suddenly realize that he is hearing a new perspective on a problem from an unexpected source. Successful leaders need to surround themselves with people who offer diverse and valuable counsel.

Successful students, too, will realize the value of such input, perhaps from friends in administration or from upperclassmen and graduates. Most will gladly give you their perspective if you ask. Do you need guidance on your academic plans? Do you need help in completing an assignment? Do you need to know how someone else met a challenge? Your answers may be found within the multitude of counselors standing ready to assist you.

Devotional focus:

A panel discussion held in Prince William County, VA, in January 2006, for college-bound high school seniors provided some invaluable insight. The college students comprising the panel came from New York, Texas, Missouri, Virginia, and West Virginia. Their schools, private and public, large and small, even included a military academy and a local community college. We thought you would like to hear some of the students' comments. Take time to reflect upon this important and practical information:

"Everyone gets homesick." * "You have to take responsibility for your room. There is no one to tell you to pick up things." * "You need to maintain your health. Sleep right, eat right, and exercise." * "I didn't fit in at first." * "Don't be isolated." * "Find your place." * "Everyone is from somewhere. Get to know people." * "Expect cultural and regional differences." * "Practice time management." * "Sometimes you have to compromise with a roommate." * "Be flexible." * "Choose your battles wisely." * "Get involved." * "Make new friends." * "Take advantage of the tutoring service if you need it." * "Get your work done." * "Practice structure and discipline." * "Never give up!"

Journal reflection:

___

___

___

___

___

___

___

___

___

___

___

___

A New Door Has Opened

Scriptural insight:

And Moses said unto the people, Remember this day, in which ye came out from Egypt, out of the house of bondage; for by strength of hand the Lord brought you out from this place. (Exodus 13:3)

Making and laying bricks ranks as one of the toughest jobs a construction worker can have. Knowing that you are a slave and feeling the sting of a whip upon your back would make construction work intolerable. Yet, this picture describes the condition of the nation of Israel before God delivered it.

Imagine the joy of Israel's people when their liberation from slavery became a reality. They fled Egypt with great jubilation. No longer would they suffer at the hands of a cruel taskmaster. Their amazing deliverance caused a song and a dance to rise from their hearts (Exodus 15).

Just before God displayed His mighty power and delivered them, He had something important to say: "Remember," He told the children of Israel. God used that one word on numerous occasions to motivate them to be thankful for what He had done for them. They were to look back and remember where they had been, to be thankful for what God had done for them.

Devotional focus:

Let me share the story of a college graduate who remembers what God did for him. It's heartbreaking to see a loved one die, yet that is what he went through as he said good-bye to his father. His father's heart condition had meant the family had no mortgage insurance, so his father's death left the family with a house payment. The student had a tremendous desire to attend college, but he knew his family needed his income to survive. He felt trapped. The door to school seemed closed and locked.

After several years, he prayed one day in desperation, asking God to deliver him. He felt entangled, he told God, as if he would never be able to pursue his dream. An answer to his prayer came quite suddenly. In his heart he heard the words, "I'll get you out of this, but remember!" The next few months brought some unexpected financial miracles. He still remembers how the impossible became a reality. He still remembers that God opened the door that had been closed for so long.

To those who may feel entangled and stuck, let me tell you that God can make a way to deliver you. To others wondering how they will ever pay for a college education, let me tell you that God can provide the needed funds. The Lord has promised to do more than we could ask or think (Ephesians 3:20). The Lord does open many exciting, new doors for us in life, but He does ask us to remember the many wonderful miracles that He provides and to have a grateful heart. Do you remember some of the ways He has already helped you?

Journal reflection:

____

____

____

____

____

____

____

____

____

____

____

Put Your Best Foot Forward

Scriptural insight:

The steps of a good man are ordered by the Lord: and he delighteth in his way. Though he fall, he shall not be utterly cast down: for the Lord upholdeth him with his hand. (Psalm 37:23-24)

Arise, walk through the land in the length of it and in the breadth of it; for I will give it unto thee. (Genesis 13:17)

The Bible talks a lot about our steps. It lets us know that the enemy set traps for David's steps (Psalm 57:6). David knew the pressure of having the enemy surround him. He talked about his steps being uncertain (Psalm 17:11). He had a keen sense of taking cautious steps as he walked through peril and danger. His writings tell us that he knew that the Lord planned and protected his steps despite his circumstances. That knowledge gave him assurance that everything would be all right.

Abraham was also a man who sensed the importance of the steps that he was taking. The Lord told him to get up and walk across the land. God promised to give him all the land that he would walk across. Those steps of Abraham were significant.

J. Ralph Brewer once wrote that an average pair of feet takes 7,000 to 8,000 steps a day. That equals at least 2.5 million steps during the course of a year, or for a 70-year-old more than 178 million steps.[1] During our lifetime, we will walk through some hard times and some happy times. It is so reassuring to know that God knows the steps that we take (Job 14:16). He will help us to take the right path and to walk toward our purpose and destiny (Psalm 37:23). He will help us to put our best foot forward.

Devotional focus:

My graduation was outdoors on a football field. I had to take some 250 steps from my seat to the principal to receive my high school diploma. School staff had planned my steps, and I proudly walked those steps. A better word for the steps I made that day, however, might be "strides." The word "stride" has to do with taking a long step forward. It speaks of taking some easy steps with confidence.

When someone is going forward, others may say, "He is making great strides."

Life, though, begins with baby steps. Did you know that a baby might fall as many as 300 times before learning to walk? Eventually, most of us learn to walk, and our steps carry us through heat, cold, rain, snow, ice, and wind, uphill and downhill. Our steps will take us through different emotional times. We will walk into weddings and graduations, into hospital rooms, and through cemeteries. Job profoundly asserted that God even "counts our steps" (Job 31:4).

Knowing that God counts our steps, plans our steps, and protects our steps should bring us enormous comfort. Remember, He has planned the new and exciting steps you are now taking. He has promised that those steps will be protected. With the Lord's help, you can take these exciting new steps in stride.

1. J. Ralph Brewer, *Sermon Resource Manual* Vol. 1, (Cleveland, TN: Pathway Press, 1987), 134.

Journal reflection:

Follow Your Dream

Scriptural insight:

By faith Moses, when he was born, was hid three months of his parents. . . . By faith Moses, when he was come to years, refused to be called the son of Pharaoh's daughter; Choosing rather to suffer affliction with the people of God, than to enjoy the pleasures of sin for a season; Esteeming the reproach of Christ greater riches than the treasures in Egypt: for he had respect unto the recompence of the reward. (Hebrews 11:23-26)

The story of Moses' life stands as one of the most exciting stories in the Bible. I am intrigued with the way that God placed him in Pharaoh's palace. I see his mother standing on the bank of the Nile River and placing the little slime-and-pitch-covered basket in the water. The basket contains her son; the waters contain man-eating crocodiles. Does she look in a certain direction and push the basket that way? Does she offer a prayer for protection? How does she come up with a plan like this?

Her little son arrives at the right place at the right time and cries at the right moment to awaken compassion in the heart of Pharaoh's daughter. She takes him, names him Moses, and raises him. God had predestined that Moses receive a good education and, eventually, be used to write the Torah.

The book of Hebrews tells us that Moses came to a critical moment in his life. He had to make a decision that meant embracing his lavish lifestyle or walking away from it and choosing to suffer with the people of God. Remaining as part of Pharaoh's family meant that he was turning his back upon what he surely recognized as his destiny.

Moses made a tough and costly decision. He followed his dream. He turned his back upon fame, position, and riches. He chose to follow the destiny that God had dictated for his life. It's true that he made some costly mistakes, but God never abandoned him. Moses spent 40 years in the wilderness learning some valuable lessons. Apparently, it took him 40 years to graduate. When he came forth from the wilderness, he moved into his destiny, and a nation was born through the miracle-working power of God.

Devotional focus:

A few people who have chosen to attend college have received a tempting vocational offer before going to school. A graduate told me about a pivotal decision he had to make before attending college. He had worked at a thriving shoe store. The owner recognized his potential and offered him the position as manager. Deep in his heart he knew what God wanted him to do, but he wrestled with the opportunity. Should he accept the position, success, and material benefits? Perhaps the generous salary could be used for some meaningful purposes. Or should he, instead, walk away from the opportunity and attend college?

He faced the owner and let him know that he had to do what the Lord had placed in his heart. Managing that store would have been God's destiny for some. For him, however, taking that position and neglecting to follow his destiny and dream would have been a disaster. His difficult decision meant he had to endure some hardships as a student for a while. Following his graduation, he received a position that had far greater influence and significance. He has never regretted making that decision that moved him into his destiny.

Journal reflection:

____

____

____

____

____

____

You Better Recognize

Scriptural insight:

But he that had received one went and digged in the earth, and hid his lord's money. (Matthew 25:18)

For a great door and effectual is opened unto me. (1 Corinthians 16:9)

Futhermore, when I came to Troas to preach Christ's gospel, and a door was opened unto me of the Lord . . . (2 Corinthians 2:12)

The parable of the talents teaches us some vital lessons. The master gave one servant five talents. He was industrious and doubled his money, as did the servant who received two talents. The servant who received one talent, however, hid the money in the earth. He had good intentions. He did not squander the money. In fact, he kept it in what he thought was a safe place. His good intentions, though, fell far short of what his master expected of him. He squandered his opportunity.

Paul recognized the importance of taking advantage of open doors. When opportunities to preach the gospel came his way, he quickly took advantage of them. Paul wasted no time or energy in trivial pursuits. He knew that doors close and opportunities disappear. So Paul made the most of every opportunity.

Devotional focus:

The sundial that stood near my dorm will be enshrined forever in my memory. Over the years, thousands of people have walked past it. Only a handful could tell you what is inscribed upon it. The powerful inscription, though only three words, left a lasting impression upon me: "Recognize your opportunities."

When we consider that most people, including some bright but poor students, will never get a chance to go to college, it makes us realize how blessed we are. Given this wonderful gift, we must make absolutely sure that we make the most of it. A few students are like the one-talent man in the parable. They simply squander the opportunity that they have received for an education.

In observing both serious and less committed students, it makes me want to ask two important questions. One, "Why are you here?" and two, "Are you taking advantage of your opportunity?" Answering the first question, those who are not serious about an education would answer, I imagine, in some surprising ways. They might struggle to tell you where they want to be in the future. Those who are serious about an education, however, would tell you quickly what degree they are seeking and probably would tell you about their future plans. To the second question, a few students would have to admit that they are letting their opportunity slip away. The vast majority, however, would tell you they are doing everything in their power to take advantage of their schooling.

How would you respond to these questions? A lot of teens today would put it this way, "You better recognize!"

Journal reflection:

____

____

____

____

____

____

____

____

____

____

Chapter Two

The Trauma of Transition

1. *Are You Ready to Stretch?*
2. *Room No. 108*
3. *Unpacking All Your Baggage*
4. *The Challenge of Transition*
5. *The Tears of Transition*
6. *The Emotional Roller Coaster*
7. *What Are You Afraid Of*

Voices and Choices

"My parents dropped me off in front of my dorm. I stood there crying. I found out later the reason they left so fast. Mom cried almost all the way home."

"My parents just left me, and I'm freaking out!"

"I feel overwhelmed. I am mortified."

"I'm having separation anxiety."

"I cried, and all the girls on my hall were crying."

"I went to school and didn't have any trouble adjusting. The school was close to home, and I commuted. My sister went away to school and cried for six months. I am the oldest, and she was the youngest. It was much harder for her."

"You've got to give it time."

Journal Focus

Whether you live on campus or at home, you have by now probably attended your first class. Try to write about the emotional changes that you are experiencing and about how well you are adjusting.

Strength Through Prayer

"Heavenly Father, help me as I attempt to get settled. Please dry my tears when I miss my family and friends. Amen."

Are You Ready to Stretch?

Scriptural insight:

Enlarge the place of thy tent, and let them stretch forth the curtains of thine habitations: spare not, lengthen thy cords, and strengthen thy stakes; for thou shalt break forth on the right hand and on the left. (Isaiah 54:2-3)

The Lord had a remarkable revelation for Israel. God was sending His people into captivity, and through this confinement they would learn a valuable lesson—that they should have no other gods before Jehovah (Exodus 20:3-5). He was speaking to them about their future and telling them that He would restore them to their homeland. God promised that they would experience His blessings and see an increase in their number. He would forgive their sins and restore His favor to them. These future events required that Israel be flexible as they experienced what God was going to do.

Jesus talked about the importance of stretching. He referred to putting new wine into brand new wineskins (Matthew 9:17). During the fermentation process, the skin would stretch. Jesus was establishing a new covenant, so He used this illustration to teach a lesson to the religious community, that they should be able to stretch with the fresh moving of God.

When you hear the word "stretching," it usually makes you think about a physical process, such as movements to make you flexible for a sporting event. We may tell someone who is cramped up to "stretch out." The word actually has several meanings. We may stretch physically, emotionally, materialistically, spiritually (1 Peter 2:2), and mentally. In the latter sense, a person may stretch his knowledge and intellect, as well as his ability to think and reason. Students know that they will be challenged and, to be successful, must be ready to stretch educationally.

Devotional focus:

Every student will have at least one professor who seems to get under his skin during his school years. To hear a student tell it, the professor dislikes him and has singled him out for abuse. Students know that they should show respect, but stress often causes them to make comments that they later regret. Word usually gets around about professors who pile on the work, and many students look for an easier path. You have probably heard remarks on your own campus about a "tough professor." The conversations may relate to the number of papers or projects he requires or how hard his tests are. Some students may advise their listeners to avoid that instructor.

Is it ever profitable to take a difficult professor? Is it always better to take one who is considered easy? Let us share some special insights about college instructors that we have learned from experience:

- A professor often pushes those in whom he sees potential and challenges those who need the most help. If you have ever endured the pain of braces and then seen the beauty of straightened teeth, you should understand the necessity of being stretched.
- A professor is neither your parent nor your pal. He should treat you fairly, but he still has a job to do.
- A professor could lower his standards to gain friends, but how would that help you later in life?
- A difficult professor may be exactly what you need.

In hindsight, we can say that the toughest professors taught us the most. Although we grumbled about them at the time, they did the best job of preparing us for the future. Now we appreciate the challenge of being stretched!

Journal reflection:

___

___

___

___

Room No. 108

Scriptural insight:

By faith Abraham, when he was called to go out into a place which he should after receive for an inheritance, obeyed. (Hebrews 11:8)

. . . and confessed that they were strangers and pilgrims on the earth. (Hebrews 11:13)

The story of Abraham's obedience and blessings, recorded throughout the pages of God's Word, shows magnificent moments of God revealing Himself and His will to Abraham. We see staggering promises that God made to Abraham. We read about those promises being fulfilled and about how God performed His Word. As a result of these covenantal promises, God literally birthed the nation of Israel.

The writer of Hebrews gives us special insight into what motivated Abraham, making us privy to what he had in his heart. Abraham, who lived in a tent, recognized that he was a pilgrim on a journey. He had a keen sense of entering into the eternity that exists beyond this life. "For he looked for a city which hath foundations, whose builder and maker is God" (Hebrews 11:10).

Devotional focus:

My simply furnished dormitory room, assigned to me on my first day of college, was No. 108. Built in 1966, my dorm held 94 male students, had three community showers, a laundry, and stood in a convenient campus location. Over the last 40 years, my room has housed about 100 men who have pursued various degrees. These men have entered a wide range of careers, and they have been influential in many walks of life. I kept no count of the number of days I spent inside those four walls and gave no thought to how quickly those days would end. I was a resident for only a short while, simply passing through. Years later when I visited the room, I had a warm and sentimental feeling about the time I had spent there.

I have traveled through many states on both local and interstate highways, often stopping to use the restroom, pick up a drink or map, and stretch my stiff legs. Some of these rest areas have been situated in scenic spots and have had nice places for travelers to sit and relax. Most have been clean, but some have been less desirable, making one almost afraid to use them.

Who would think that a rest area would trigger any spiritual thoughts? Yet, I often think about Abraham when I make such a stop. It reminds me that life on earth is temporary, just as Abraham said. I've never attempted to hang a picture in a rest area or to have my mail sent there, as the stop lasts but a short time. That's just how life is.

Room No. 108 provided the necessary shelter as I worked to obtain my degree. No plaque hangs there announcing that I was once a resident. My stay was temporary. As you sit, study, and sleep in your room, you should remember that you are there to be challenged and stretched, to receive your degree, and to develop tools necessary to become successful. Your dorm room illustrates a stop on your journey through life, so make the most of it.

Journal reflection:

Unpacking All Your Baggage

Scriptural insight:

Casting all your care upon him; for he careth for you. (1 Peter 5:7)

For we have not an high priest which cannot be touched with the feeling of our infirmities. (Hebrews 4:15)

We have an advocate with the Father, Jesus Christ the righteous. (1 John 2:1)

Doctors, psychologists, and ministers all have solutions when it comes to examining and diagnosing your problems. Once they address your medical, psychological, or spiritual needs, they may offer advice, prescribe medication, refer you to a specialist, or help you using spiritual means.

Self-help books try to point you to your problem and offer remedies. You are likely to learn about chemical imbalances, family dysfunction, unresolved issues from childhood abuse, and attention deficit disorder. Your problems may stem from any number of sources.

Lots of people decide to secretly and silently carry a hidden problem without seeking any type of help. To those suffering secretly, let me ask you these questions. Have you identified your struggles? Have you prayerfully considered what might be causing your anger? Do you know why you dislike yourself? How can you get better? Going to the Lord in prayer is a good place to start. The Bible tells us that Jesus cares about us. He feels the pain that you may be experiencing. He represents you as a High Priest, and He prays for your needs. He tells you to cast your cares (abuse, hurts, wounds, pain, rejection, resentment, and sins) upon Him in prayer. Healing quite often comes as you forgive others who have wronged you.

Devotional focus:

Watch freshmen move into a dorm and you will often find it both intriguing and entertaining. You'll see sweaty brows and tired expressions, and you will wonder: How did they get all those boxes into the car? What could they possibly contain? How many trips have they had to make to get their possessions here? Have they tried to bring everything from their room at home? Where are they going to put all that baggage?

Whole families stand and gaze at the dorm room. Everyone has ideas about how to place items in the room or whether to store them. Roommates usually work together eagerly to find room for all their belongings. Parents find themselves returning home with some items and wondering why their child had taken them to school in the first place.

Of course, you can decide whether to unload your physical belongings, but some baggage you bring stays packed up. As a student, you may carry with you emotional and spiritual problems that you need to resolve before you can grow, take this exciting step, or meet these new challenges. Why not ask the Lord to take these burdens off your shoulders? Let God help you, and start this new phase in your life free of all that baggage.

Journal reflection:

___

___

___

___

___

___

___

___

___

The Challenge of Transition

Scriptural insight:

As I was with Moses, so I will be with thee: I will not fail thee, nor forsake thee. Be strong and of a good courage. (Joshua 1:5-6)

. . . that ye may know the way by which ye must go: for ye have not passed this way heretofore. (Joshua 3:4)

Joshua had served as an apprentice and was like a student to Moses. He had been second in charge for many years. Now, all of Israel was in mourning. Moses had passed away, leaving Joshua in command. Assisting Moses was one thing, but being the man in charge was quite another. As Joshua assumed the role as leader of Israel, his mind must have been plagued with doubts and questions.

Joshua faced a demanding new beginning. Israel was in a state of transition, and the future seemed uncertain. Suddenly, in the midst of his mourning and misgivings, God spoke to him. He told Joshua to be strong and to have courage; He would be with him as he braved the future. Joshua could handle the challenges of transition knowing that God had promised to be at his side.

Devotional focus:

Just prior to leaving for school, you filled your days with shopping, packing, and saying good-bye to family and friends. Your last night at home in your bed was spent tossing and turning. Questions about the future persisted into the night and left you exhausted the next morning. Listen to these freshmen as they share their feelings of anxiety while moving into a dorm for the first time:

"I feel overwhelmed!"
"I am mortified!"
"I'm freaking out!"
"I've got to make myself calm down!"

I believe the comforting words that God spoke to the troubled heart of Joshua are vital when facing a difficult change. He told

Joshua to be strong and to have courage. He reassured him that He would be with him as he faced this tough move.

Choosing a major, having a roommate, making new friends, and beginning classes may overwhelm you. Knowing that God stands with you should bring you comfort and strength to face this new adventure in life.

Journal reflection:

The Tears of Transition

Scriptural insight:

Put my tears into thy bottle: are they not in thy book? (Psalm 56:8)

I am weary with my groaning; all the night make I my bed to swim; I water my couch with tears. (Psalm 6:6)

And stood at his feet behind him weeping, and began to wash his feet with tears, and did wipe them with the hairs of her head. (Luke 7:38)

Serving the Lord with all humility of mind, and with many tears. (Acts 20:19)

Who in the days of his flesh, when he had offered up prayers and supplications with strong crying and tears. (Hebrews 5:7)

The Bible never makes any attempt to hide its characters' tears. Most of us, however, feel ashamed if anyone discovers that we've been crying. People differ emotionally. Some students adjust quickly to school, rarely weeping, while others struggle and cry incessantly.

The Scriptures above represent a sample of the Bible's references to tears and crying. The Bible frankly tells us that Jesus wept. Paul admits in Scripture to crying. David, whose tears flowed often, even wrote about his tears in songs. The woman who washed Jesus' feet wept openly before others. The Bible refers frequently to tears as part of living.

Indeed, both laughter and tears fill our lives daily. We laugh, for instance, at jokes, at parties and weddings, and with special friends. Our tears fall in times of sadness, perhaps because we feel homesick, lonely, isolated, or stressed. We should never try to hide our happiness or tears. Jesus didn't!

Devotional focus:

Dr. Paul Conn once spoke to a group of parents and potential students at Lee University in Cleveland, Tennessee. I'll always remember his comment about adjusting to college life. "I cried a bucketful of tears," he said. Admitting to a difficult transition, he made an honest revelation about what most college students can expect.

A freshmen girl beginning her education at a Virginia school said, "I was crying, and the whole hall was crying." She told me that her tears later dried up and that she enjoyed college life.

Change always generates doubts, fears, and questions. So, naturally, the first day of school for freshmen or returning students brings a bundle of anxiety. New students revealing their feelings to me about moving into a dorm and facing transition used the word "tears" more than any other.

Those who have survived this move want you to know that the tears will eventually stop, and you will endure the transition. You may think that you will need a bucket to catch your tears, but time will reveal that you hardly needed a tissue.

Journal reflection:

The Emotional Roller Coaster

Scriptural insight:

But many of the priests and Levites and chief of the fathers, who were ancient men, that had seen the first house, when the foundation of this house was laid before their eyes, wept with a loud voice; and many shouted aloud for joy. (Ezra 3:12)

The crowd that stood there had all witnessed the same events. They saw the arrival of a man named "Nehemiah." They heard him talk about his dream. They witnessed his passion to rebuild the temple and the wall around the city. They saw him endure hard times and watched as persecution enveloped his life. Some had helped remove debris left after the Babylonian soldiers invaded. Many had taken part in the rebuilding effort. Now, they stood together and viewed the finished product. The grueling task had finally come to an end.

As the dedication service progressed, mixed emotions ran through the crowd. Some wept as they remembered the old temple. Some cried out with joy as they admired the new temple. Some felt depressed as they compared the new temple to the old one. Some voiced enthusiasm at now having a temple for worship.

Today, any given crowd of people will have a mixture of thoughts and emotions. Take, for instance, a company setting. A retiring worker may feel sad; his replacement, exhilarated. Look at a classroom. Someone feels excited about a good grade on a test; another student, dejected because he blew it. Even within a worship service, we find mixed emotions. One member of a congregation may have had excruciating pain recently, while another person may have experienced a miraculous blessing. A roller coaster is a good example to help us reflect on the twists and turns of people's emotions.

Devotional focus:

Mixed emotions run rampant on a college campus as the school year begins. We've witnessed some parents dropping off their child with laughter and joy, others, with tears. Some students watch with excitement as their parents pull away from the parking lot. They can hardly wait to be on their own. Others cry and feel separation anxiety as their parents' car fades from view. Some students enjoy being in a dorm, while others hate the arrangement. Some love the cafeteria food; others avoid it.

A student's emotional journey may be likened to a roller coaster ride, with its highs and lows. You'll encounter both straight ways and hard curves. Some days you'll weep, but you'll also laugh. At times you will enjoy the freedom of being on your own; other times, you will be homesick for your family. Did you know you could learn lessons from a roller coaster ride?

- Some people are too afraid to ride a roller coaster. You must never let fear paralyze you or deprive you of taking a new and exciting journey.
- Some people enjoy the thrill of the ride, while others cry. We all have different emotions as we encounter the highs and lows of life.
- Some people feel like it is the end of the world, while others never want the ride to end. We all view things very differently in life.
- Everyone has to hang on for dear life at times. Every student will have similar challenges.
- It's good to ride one with a friend. All of us need a friend who can help us through the ups and downs.
- Remember that the ride is only temporary and ends before you know it. Don't lose the perspective that college life will be over sooner than you can imagine.
- People usually exit a roller coaster and look back with a good memory. You may have some pain now, but later you will have many fond memories of school. Enjoy the ride!

Journal reflection:

____

____

____

What Are You Afraid Of?

Scriptural insight:

I will not be afraid of ten thousands of people. (Psalm 3:6)

The Lord is my light and my salvation; whom shall I fear. (Psalm 27:1)

What time I am afraid, I will trust in thee. (Psalm 56:3)

I will fear no evil: for thou art with me. (Psalm 23:4)

David, who was a man on the run, feared for his life. King Saul had ordered his elite soldiers to find and destroy him. Jealousy drove the king, because the people admired David more than they did him. The soldiers knew that David's death meant promotion, fame, and riches for them, so they took their mission seriously. David had many close calls and was hemmed in several times while trying to elude them.

His narrow escapes brought fear to David and moved him to write about it in many of his songs. In the midst of his apprehension, he wrote that he trusted God. He rested in the assurance that God would protect him, and that God would calm all of his anxiety.

Devotional focus:

Our fears have about 600 different clinical names. We call a fear of heights "acrophobia," of being closed in "claustrophobia," of change "tropophobia," and of thunderstorms "astraphobia." And we call the fear of spiders "arachnophobia," of blushing "erythrophobia," and of sermons "homilophobia." You get the picture.

Scary scenes in movies and television exploit our fears, causing faster and deeper breaths, more rapid heartbeats, nervous behavior, and sweaty palms. Fear can make you sick. It can even put you into the hospital.

Leaving home, moving into a dorm, and starting new classes, all part of beginning a new life as a student can sometimes paralyze students with fear. When I asked a freshman from Virginia about his first few days of school, he said, "I am petrified!" Another student in Tennessee said, "I am scared to death!" New students should understand that such feelings, though they do increase our stress level, are normal. One young lady knew what she had to do, and her action serves as a good example for other students. "I had to calm myself down," she said.

What scares you? Do you need to calm down? Do you realize that the Lord stands with you and that He strengthens you to face whatever tomorrow may bring? Take a deep breath. Slow down. Relax. You made it through orientation and your first day of class. You're settled in your dorm room. Your fears will soon subside.

Paul reminded those who have a fear factor that through the Lord he could accomplish anything. He said, "I can do all things through Christ which strengtheneth me" (Philippians 4:13). And you can too.

Journal reflection:

Chapter Three

Facing Initial Challenges

1. *Great Expectations*
2. *Freedom, Fun, and a Future*
3. *Helping Your Parents Adjust*
4. *Utilizing Campus Resources*
5. *The Voice That Matters Most*
6. *Two Thousand Six Hundred Eighty-Eight Hours*
7. *What Are You Looking At?*

Voices and Choices

"I set myself up for failure. I got off to a bad start by living off-campus with four friends. They influenced me to make some bad decisions. I made some dumb mistakes and had to start all over later."

"If I were starting school now, I would ask more questions."

"Don't forget to talk to your counselor. His job is to help you."

"Take advantage of the tutoring service, if you need it."

"Try to get organized as soon as possible."

"You will find what you are looking for at school."

"Don't get lost along the way."

Journal Focus

Try to write your thoughts and plans about getting a good start in school. How can you become proactive about any adjustments that you need to make in order to achieve a good, new beginning?

Strength Through Prayer

"Dear Lord, I recognize that I am facing a lot of new demands and will have to modify my life. Please help me to see what areas I need to alter, and give me the strength to get a good start this semester. Amen."

Great Expectations

Scriptural insight:

My soul, wait thou only upon God; for my expectation is from him. (Psalm 62:5)

So shall the knowledge of wisdom be unto thy soul: when thou hast found it, then there shall be a reward, and thy expectation shall not be cut off. (Proverbs 24:14)

An expectation resembles a prelude, which prepares an audience for a service, wedding, or show that's about to start. The word "expectation" as used in Scripture refers to anticipation. For example, the children of Israel looked forward expectantly to their great feasts, festivals, and special days marking events in the nation's history.

To have expectation means to have hope. We expect and hope, for instance, to be successful and happy. Expectation also comprises a vital part of the Christian life. As children of God, we expect Him to answer prayer. We expect God to strengthen us and give us the ability to meet the demands of life. We expect to see the Lord at the end of this life. Expectation is the fruit and the byproduct of having faith in God.

Devotional focus:

For those who enter college, the word "expectation" may have both negative and positive connotations. I've seen freshmen who arrive expecting college to be heaven on earth, while others envision the opposite. Truth to tell, you will find what you expect. Of course, some students arrive with no clue as to what awaits them. Unrealistic expectations often breed disappointment and disillusionment. Here are some questions to help you to establish a realistic framework as you begin or continue your college education:

1. *Do you believe that every student wants to be there?* In reality, some students attend school only to please parents who have saved for years to send them to college. These young adults will most likely forfeit this grand opportunity and make others feel miserable in the process.

2. *Do you expect college life to be without challenges or disappointments?* Many students seem surprised and overwhelmed when they encounter a few setbacks, but hindrances should teach valuable lessons about resilience.
3. *Do you think that everyone will live in harmony with no personality conflicts or misunderstandings?* Quite often roommates struggle to get along. It takes work to make dorm life tolerable. Though you will forge some lasting friendships, some people will simply get on your last nerve.

These three simple questions serve as a good place to start in helping you to see the difference between your expectations and reality. You should be realistic and maintain a positive outlook to avoid feeling frustrated. At this exciting time in your life, you might ask yourself what good things you expect to happen in your future. Why not make a list of some of your positive expectations. This exercise will help you to clarify your goals.

Journal reflection:

____

____

____

____

____

____

____

____

____

Freedom, Fun, and a Future

Scriptural insight:

Stand fast therefore in the liberty wherewith Christ hath made us free, and be not entangled again with the yoke of bondage. (Galatians 5:1)

Jesus Christ gave us spiritual freedom from the slavery of sin. Shortly after He prayed in the garden, the soldiers bound Him physically. Shortly after He went to the cross, He loosed us spiritually.

Paul talked often about the freedom that Jesus provided. He wrote, "Sin shall not have dominion over you" (Romans 6:14). He also said, "Ye were the servants of sin" (Romans 6:17). He revealed to us that salvation "made [us] free from sin" (Romans 6:18). So when the church at Galatia started reverting to some of its old ways, he warned the people and advised them to stand firmly in the liberty that Jesus had provided.

When old friends call and tempt you to go back to your old ways, tell them about your new life, and that you choose to stay free of sin.

Devotional focus:

A trip to the library or cinema may provide you with either a horror story or a happy story. But, truly, both kinds of stories may be found not just at those places, but also in our everyday lives. Without being too negative, let's look at people right around us who have misused their independence. Students who leave home for college experience a lack of certain restrictions for the first time. No one tells them when to come home, clean their room, or go to bed. No one tells them how to drive, who they should choose for friends, or where they can go. Some students handle the situation well, making wise decisions. For others, the taste of independence clouds their judgment. We've witnessed painful events that you should hear to help you understand the consequences of a poor decision:

- She wanted to experiment with sex for the first time. She later discovered that she was pregnant and had to drop out of school.
- He wanted to enjoy a sexual encounter. He discovered that he had AIDS.
- She wanted to get drunk. An auto accident put her into a coma. Her body shriveled away, and she died in her early 20s.
- One boy, who had suffered a coma, told an audience that he had drunk himself silly on the night of his prom and wrecked his car. He will spend the rest of his life in a wheelchair. He pleaded with high school students to make good decisions.
- A young woman hung out with the wrong people and went to the wrong places. She became a rape victim.

We want you to know that your freedom gives you the opportunity to make decisions and choices that have lasting effects. Have fun, but avoid jeopardizing your future. You will write your own life story—make it a happy one.

Journal reflection:

____

____

____

____

____

____

____

____

Helping Your Parents Adjust

Scriptural insight:

When Jesus therefore saw his mother, and the disciple standing by, whom he loved, he saith unto his mother, Woman, behold thy son! Then saith he to the disciple, Behold thy mother! And from that hour that disciple took her unto his own home. (John 19:26-27)

Anguish filled the final moments of Jesus' life. He offered Himself up to God as a sacrifice for the sins of man, a substitute for us. We can read the seven final statements that Jesus made in the four Gospels. He prayed that God would forgive those who crucified Him. He prayed to His Father as He felt distanced from God because of our sins. He promised a repentant thief that he would enter paradise. He told those around Him that He was thirsty. He commended His Spirit back to God. He cried, "It is finished," (John 19:30), a legal term meaning He had paid our sin debt in full, thus completing the salvation plan. Many have read the Scriptures without noticing the seventh statement He made from the cross.

As Jesus suffered, He looked down and saw His mother, Mary, looking up at Him and weeping. With a breaking heart, she watched her son dying. She had carried this son, conceived of the Holy Ghost, in her womb for nine months. Then, He had made her proud with His miracles and fame throughout all of Palestine. Though Jesus carried the weight of the world's sins, He prayed for the soldiers and loved a thief. And He remembered His mother. Looking at John, He told him to care for His mother. Following the crucifixion, she went to John's home to live. Even while dying, Jesus felt an obligation to her.

Devotional focus:

Freshmen often leave home eagerly to begin a life on their own. No one will be there to tell them to pick up clothes, do laundry, take out trash, or make the bed. During the first weeks of college, phone calls will fly back and forth, with parents checking on their son or daughter's welfare. The student tends to call when he encounters a problem or feels homesick. Soon, both parents and student must get used to living separate lives. That's when mom and dad begin to miss their kid. They often go through deep depression. They cope with the empty room and the empty chair at dinner and try to prepare smaller meals. Less laughter fills the home. Parents struggle to adjust at home, just as students do at school.

That's why students should help their parents through the changes. No matter how many assignments, projects, or parties you have, stay in touch. Your chat may be brief, but they need to hear from you. The sound of your voice will brighten their day and lift their spirits. Also, try to keep track of family members' birthdays, and go home for holidays. Remember those who always have you uppermost in their thoughts.

Journal reflection:

___

___

___

___

___

___

___

___

___

___

___

Utilizing Campus Resources

Scriptural insight:

And it came to pass, that after three days they found him in the temple, sitting in the midst of the doctors, both hearing them, and asking them questions. (Luke 2:46)

This Bible story makes us want to ask some questions of our own. How did the family of Jesus fail to notice that He was missing? Why did it take three days to locate Him? Why did Jesus sit in the midst of doctors rather than in a location that most young men would have preferred? Part of the answers relate to how families and friends in Bible times traveled together to Jerusalem for protection and fellowship. They felt safer with a group and could catch up on any news.

A whole travel day had elapsed before they discovered that Jesus was missing. What a shock, and how difficult and sleepless must have been the night for Joseph and Mary. It took them three days of searching, but they found Jesus with the doctors in the temple, posing questions to them. When Mary asked, "Son, why have you dealt with us this way?" Jesus responded with two questions. "Why were you looking for me? Don't you know that I must be about my Father's business?"

Jesus sat asking questions. Mary and Joseph arrived asking questions. Jesus responded with questions.

Devotional focus:

The university junior had good advice to share with those beginning their undergraduate journey. "If I were starting school now, I would ask more questions," he said. Then, he talked about colleges and universities providing personnel to answer questions for new students, and said that he regretted his failure to take advantage of that vast knowledge and experience when he was a freshman. "Many upperclassmen would gladly help new students, if they would only ask. We could share lessons from the things that we have learned," he said.

Certainly, many upperclassmen prefer to be left alone. Even some school employees seem too preoccupied to assist. Nevertheless, many staff members will make time for you, if they know you need them. Some knowledgeable people eagerly await your questions and would enjoy helping you. Remember to utilize the knowledge, experience, and resources of others when you have questions. Someone once said, "You'll never know unless you ask!" After you ask a question, someone might say, "I'm glad that you asked!"

One student told us that the most popular place on her campus was a building provided for students to study around the clock. It had wireless Internet, food, tutoring, and other resources for them. Her advice for new students: Ask questions and remember to take advantage of the resources on campus.

Journal reflection:

The Voice That Matters Most

Scriptural insight:

If they have persecuted me, they will also persecute you. (John 15:20)

And a man's foes shall be they of his own household. (Matthew 10:36)

Jesus made some startling statements about opposition in the Bible. He let us know that we can expect opposition and persecution in the Christian life. We certainly see resistance to the ministry of Jesus. Religious groups opposed him. Political organizations opposed him. At times, even His friends and family opposed Him. For instance, in one shocking incident that occurred in the life of Jesus, His friends literally tried to "lay hold" of Him physically, thinking that he had lost His mind (Mark 3:21). They misunderstood who He was and what God wanted Him to accomplish.

Another outrageous example, recorded in the Gospel of St. John, transpired in Jerusalem during feast time. By this time in His ministry, Jesus was drawing much undesirable attention from the religious establishment, whose members sought to kill Him. His own brothers tried to provoke Him into showing himself openly and thus endangering His life (John 7:1-5). The hostility and harassment against Him eventually became so strong that those who hated Him constantly challenged His teachings. Jesus gave us a shining example of strength and resolve in the face of opposition. He refused to let anyone deter Him from doing the will of God, thus pleasing His Father. His family did come to believe in Him a little later.

Devotional focus:

Your decision to attend college or to pursue the direction that you have prayerfully chosen may elicit mixed emotions from family and friends. Most will rejoice over your choice and encourage you; a few will oppose your choice and discourage you.

While attending college, I rarely had enough money to eat out, so I went to the cafeteria almost every day. I sat from time to time near different people and heard discussions on a variety of topics, such as classes, tests, professors, and research papers. Occasionally, a student would open up and tell a surprising story, revealing that many of them knew about voices that opposed, ridiculed, and attacked because of the choice they had made. Many knew the constant barrage of verbal assaults before leaving for college. One young lady told of being severely criticized by her grandmother for going away to a Christian college. I even heard two young men talk of being disinherited for choosing to attend a Christian college.

Criticism, ridicule, and opposition cause tears, bewilderment, and doubts. Like Jesus, students must exhibit strength and resolve as they hear these voices. If you know that you have selected the right college, then refuse to allow anyone to hinder you. After all, the voice that matters the most is the Voice that directed you to the right place!

Journal reflection:

Two Thousand Six Hundred Eighty-Eight Hours

Scriptural insight:

See then that ye walk circumspectly, not as fools, but as wise, Redeeming the time, because the days are evil. (Ephesians 5:15-16)

Paul reminds us that we should use care in the way we live our lives, taking advantage of our opportunities and using our time wisely. The Bible talks about our life and about time in many ways. Here are a few brief examples:

> "My times are in your hands" (Psalm 31:15).
>
> "My days are swifter than a weaver's shuttle" (Job 7:6).
>
> "For what is your life? It is even a vapour, that appeareth for a little time, and then vanisheth away" (James 4:14).
>
> "So teach us to number our days, that we may apply our hearts unto wisdom" (Psalm 90:12).

Our life, days, and even our hours come as a gift from God. Let's look at the brevity of life. If we live to be 70 years old, we have only 25,550 days, or 613,200 hours, or 36,792,000 minutes.

Students might be interested in hearing how long it takes to earn a high school diploma. Thirteen years of school equals 2,353 days, 14,118 hours, or about 8.5 million seconds. Minutes, hours, and days are priceless. Older senior adults often say, "Where did all the time go?" We must be good stewards of our time. We must be careful how we use it. One day it will certainly be used up!

Devotional focus:

Most colleges and universities call the time period for completing a course "a semester." Of course, other schools divide their year into quarters. Either way, a course requires the same amount of time. A 16-week semester of 24-hour days totals 2,688 hours. Preparing for tests, attending classes, and writing term papers sure make it seem a lot longer. If a class lasts only one hour and meets three times a week for 16 weeks, then that takes 48 hours of class time. For that one class, you earn three semester hours of credit. To earn an undergraduate degree, you must take and pass 130 semester hours—that's 2,080 hours of class time. It sure seems a lot longer. Lots of students have said, "I really wasted a lot of time in college." Lack of discipline in time management can often prove catastrophic.

How do you spend your time? Do you squander countless hours on video or computer games, texting friends, sports, dating, socializing, and other activities? Just recently, we learned that some of these things have become an addiction for many students. Educators warn students that this addiction may adversely impact their grades.

We all need leisure time, whether we're playing games or sports, dating or simply socializing. These activities help us to relax and to achieve a balance, but allocating our time foolishly to pursue mostly fun will bring disastrous results. To be successful, you must use your time wisely. Think about how much time you now spend on various activities. Are you disciplined enough to allocate 48 hours to complete the class time needed for a course? Are you disciplined enough to get out of bed and force yourself to study? The 2,688 hours for this semester will pass in a flash. How many of those hours will you dedicate to the process of becoming successful?

Journal reflection:

____

____

____

____

____

____

____

What Are You Looking At?

Scriptural insight:

And I went out by night by the gate of the valley, even before the dragon well, and to the dung port, and viewed the walls of Jerusalem, which were broken down, and the gates thereof were consumed with fire. Then I went on to the gate of the fountain, and to the king's pool: but there was no place for the beast that was under me to pass. (Nehemiah 2:13-14)

Visionaries see things that others miss. Long ago, after an invasion left Jerusalem devastated, thousands of people in Jerusalem went about their daily tasks, paying little heed to the destruction. A man named "Nehemiah," however, heard about the damage to the city and immediately began to visualize its repair. He was a visionary.

We first see Nehemiah weeping after hearing about the condition of his homeland (Nehemiah 1:3-4). Then, he gained the King's permission and traveled back home to rebuild and repair. Once there, he surveyed the terrible wreckage at night. He saw the rubble, but he looked beyond it to the beauty of what could be. He organized the people and set to work. The enemy opposed his efforts nearly every step of the way. Even so, we see him enduring and finishing the task (Nehemiah 6:15).

Another Bible story tells us about 10 men who saw only potential problems and difficulties. They numbered among the 12 spies that Moses had sent to assess the land of Canaan. Ten felt pessimistic, doubtful, and fearful of defeat. The other two showed optimism, confidence, and anticipation of victory. All 12 had witnessed God's mighty, miracle-working power and had heard God promise them mighty, military victories. Somehow, only two proved to be visionaries (Numbers 13:26-33), and only those two lived to see their vision become a reality. Doubts can kill dreams.

Devotional focus:

Let us ask you a question about being a visionary. What do you see when you try to visualize your future? Before you answer, let me tell you about our image of you. We see you at an exciting time in your life, with a wonderful opportunity in your grasp and, if you apply yourself, a bright future ahead. We glimpse your incredible potential for enormous success. So, then, what do you see?

A farmer who notices only weeds and ignores his plants will never reap a harvest. An auto body technician who sees only wreckage without visualizing a repaired car would be useless. Someone who accepts a rose and talks about the size of the thorns has missed the gift of beauty. We must use our ability to look beyond doubts and fears. A negative mindset will cause a pessimistic attitude.

What's your outlook? Are you focusing on the difficulty of your tests and papers? Are you looking at your distance from home? Are you thinking only about your sacrifices and difficulties? Are you calculating how much your education is costing? Focusing on responsibilities and challenges is normal. Nehemiah did too, but he looked beyond those hurdles.

You should be a visionary, not only seeing your current accomplishments, but also picturing what lies ahead. Be among those who allow themselves to dream and accomplish great things. Cultivate and cherish your dream, realizing that every class you attend brings you closer to its realization.

Journal reflection:

____

____

____

____

____

____

____

Chapter Four

The Value of Community and Diversity

1. *Individuality, Diversity, and Community*
2. *A Roommate's Bill of Rights*
3. *Friendship 101*
4. *When Your Suitemate Is Not Sweet*
5. *When the Melting Pot Boils*
6. *Evaluating Your Friendships*
7. *Conflict Resolution 101*

Voices and Choices

"I am from Nepal. I'm going to a university in Virginia this fall to become a medical doctor. I've always been with my family, never on my own. This concerns me. I don't want to party; I wasn't raised that way. This concerns me also."

"Make new friends."

"The biggest problem I faced was finding friends I could confide in."

"Sometimes you have to compromise with a roommate."

"Be careful who you chose for friends. You can find what you are looking for at school."

Journal Focus

Record some journal entries about your progress in making friends and adapting.

Strength Through Prayer

"Dear Heavenly Father, help me to get out of my comfort zone and reach out to others for friendship. On the flip side, help me to be available to those who need someone to listen. Amen."

Individuality, Diversity, and Community

Scriptural insight:

Before I formed thee in the belly, I knew thee. (Jeremiah 1:5)

For as the body is one, and hath many members, and all the members of that one body, being many, are one body: so also is Christ. For by one Spirit are we all baptized into one body, whether we be Jews or Gentiles, whether we be bond or free; and have been all made to drink into one Spirit. For the body is not one member, but many. (1Corinthians 12:12-14)

If you ever do any traveling, you will immediately see diversity. But often you will see diversity right where you live. Even within a small group, members' traits vary widely. This was the case for Paul, who faced the challenge of bringing unity to the church at Corinth (1 Corinthians 12- 14). He strived to teach them of their oneness in Christ. He talked about different leadership positions (Ephesians 4:11), different gifts (Romans 12:3-8), and even different eating habits within the church (Romans 14:1-3). Of course, financial levels ranged from poor to wealthy. In pointing out diversity, Paul reinforced the need for unity within this community. We often refer to a university or college as "a community," which defines a group of people sharing, working, and living in a unified environment. We also refer to the university or college we graduate from as our "alma mater." This Latin term further illustrates community in an even greater way. Those words mean, "nourishing mother."

Devotional focus:

As we entered a shopping mall one day, we noticed two young teenagers walking past us. They really stood out from the crowd. One young man had his hair painted red; the other, green. Both had spiked hair that stood about eight inches above their heads. They walked together, obviously enjoying all the attention that others were paying them. I saw another hard-to-believe sight at a different shopping location. There, a young woman had 15 piercings on one ear alone. All kinds of objects weighed down her ears. Everyone who passed her took notice.

In today's world, many people use extreme means to express themselves. They may pierce and tattoo their bodies. They may grow their hair long, shave it, spike it, or paint it. They may wear skimpy, baggy, torn, or faded clothing. They may buy auto hubcaps that spin or light up. All this diversity cries, "I'm unique. No one else is like me. Notice me. Give me some attention." People striving to be different really just want the crowd to accept them. Lots of students strive to be noticed through the Internet. MySpace and Facebook are very popular methods that many students use to express themselves.

Torn clothes, tight clothes, baggy clothes, bright clothes, faded clothes, body piercing, tattoos, no hair, long hair, shaved hair, painted hair, spiked hair, spinning hubcaps, Facebook, and MySpace may fail to garner you any attention. Nor may your abilities, activities, and achievements bring recognition your way. But one thing remains certain: God knows exactly who you are. He reminded Jeremiah that He knew him before he was even born. Scriptures remind us that He knows our thoughts. He has ordered the steps for our lives. He even knows the hairs of our head (green, red, spiked, or long). He knows us better then we know ourselves. He loves us and accepts us as special individuals.

Journal reflection:

____

____

____

____

____

____

____

A Roommate's Bill of Rights

Scriptural insight:

Forbearing one another, and forgiving one another, if any man have a quarrel against any: even as Christ forgave you, so also do ye. (Colossians 3:13)

With all lowliness and meekness, with longsuffering, forbearing one another in love; Endeavouring to keep the unity of the Spirit in the bond of peace. (Ephesians 4:2-3)

The early church occasionally had some difficulties. Epistles of the New Testament stand as a reminder of the many and varied problems that existed within the young church. Divisions and jealousy appeared within the church at Corinth, and Paul dealt with the discord in a powerful way, addressing jealousy, selfishness, confusion, and even immorality (1 Corinthians 12-14). He called upon believers to solve these problems through love (1 Corinthians 13).

Paul's letters spoke of love, unity, and forgiveness within the church. He recognized that a disagreement, or even a difference of opinion, could lead to serious consequences. So Paul pleaded with them to have patience with each other, forgiving one another when an offense occurred. He continually stressed the importance of loving others within the body of Christ. He knew that patience, longsuffering, and forgiveness would lead to a unified body of believers. The person who offends you the most may be the exact person who often needs your patience and prayers.

Devotional focus:

Two eight-year-old boys were playing videos games during free time at a youth camp. One moment they were getting along fine; the next, they were fighting. We separated them, but expected them to go at it again. The next thing that happened, however, startled all of us. Within ten minutes, they were playing the game together as if nothing had happened. They had forgiven each other and moved on. I thought, "I wish adults could learn to be like these two kids."

Make no mistake about it, a dormitory can be a breeding ground for disagreements, and hard feelings arise in a flash. Living together in close proximity brings out the worst in some and the best in others. One important guideline should direct all those who find themselves living with total strangers: Respect the rights of others! Our founding fathers wrote a document called the "Bill of Rights" that reminds us that our nation has many wonderful freedoms. Though written for our nation, this document's principles work even within a smaller setting, such as a dorm room.

As a roommate, you should recognize the rights of others. Each of you paid for half of the room. No title deed exists to show that the room belongs to either one of you. You will maintain peace only as you learn to forgive, have patience, give space, model respect, and show love toward your roommate and dorm neighbors. Here's a scary thought: How would you feel if you had a roommate who was just like you? What effort have you put into becoming your roommate's friend? Do you understand anything about his journey before you met him? Have you considered his feelings? Are you showing him the respect that you expect? Have you recognized that he has rights too?

Journal reflection:

____

____

____

____

____

____

____

____

Friendship 101

Scriptural insight:

A friend loveth at all times, and a brother is born for adversity. (Proverbs 17:17)

Iron sharpeneth iron; so a man sharpeneth the countenance of his friend. (Proverbs 27:17)

Two are better than one; because they have a good reward for their labour. For if they fall, the one will lift up his fellow. (Ecclesiastes 4:9-10)

An auto mechanic works hard, as does a painter and a plumber. Scores of tough occupations require both physical and mental stamina, yet many of our most demanding jobs render no financial compensation. Friendship serves as a good example. For instance:

- In real friendship, we love others at all times, even through hurts and disappointments.
- In real friendship, we speak the truth to others, even though they may resent it.
- In real friendship, we often hold our peace and resist the urge to interfere.
- None of us ever has enough friends.
- None of us knows when we might make new and lasting friendships.
- All of us must work to maintain friendships.
- Friends will do what is best for us; we will do what is best for them.

Any relationship will encounter misunderstandings, differences of opinion, and conflicting ideas. These situations represent a good test of our friendship. How do we react at these times? Have you ever heard of someone failing a friendship test? It might have sounded like this: "I'll never speak to that person again as long as I live!" The Bible reminds us that, "A friend loveth at all times" (Proverbs 17:17). Even when a friend hurts us, rejects us, or makes hurtful comments to us, we must love that person and refrain from hurting them in return. "A soft answer turneth away wrath: but grievous words stir up anger" (Proverbs 15:1).

Devotional focus:

As you enter a college classroom the first day of school, your professor will usually hand you a syllabus, which communicates the expectations and requirements that you must meet to successfully complete the course. If there were a syllabus for a class on friendship, it would probably look like this:

"Friendship 101 is an entry-level course for all those who want to excel in such camaraderie. This class has no professor, nor does it meet at a specific time or in a specific location. It requires no written papers. To pass this course, you must forgive your friends when they mistreat you. You must treat them with love even though they act heartless. You must show kindness when they are cruel. You must respect them even as they hold you in low regard. Completing this course will enable you to maintain lifelong friendships."

Journal reflection:

When Your Suitemate Is Not Sweet

Scriptural insight:

For it was not an enemy that reproached me; then I could have borne it: neither was it he that hated me that did magnify himself against me; then I would have hid myself from him: But it was thou, a man mine equal, my guide, and mine acquaintance. We took sweet counsel together, and walked unto the house of God in company. (Psalm 55:12-14)

These verses came from a greatly wounded heart. It was David's heart, and his trusted friend, Ahithophel, caused the wounds. David had shared both friendship and worship with Ahithophel. He had even received special counsel from this trusted advisor. 2 Samuel 15-18 tells this tragic story.

How they became friends or how long their friendship lasted remains a mystery. Nor do we know how many times they worshiped together or discussed what was best for the nation of Israel. But we do know that they were close, and that Ahithophel held a special place in David's heart. When a rebellion came against the house of David, Ahithophel turned against the king, even giving counsel on how to kill him. When those in revolt ignored his advice, Ahithophel took his own life.

Following the uprising, we can see David asking questions about his comrade. The answers must have astonished him. How could his friend have turned on him so abruptly? David must have been stunned at the news that his friend wanted him dead. His wounded heart reflects his pain in Psalm 55. David regained his throne after the rebellion. Gradually, he healed emotionally from the pain of the insurgence and all its terrible consequences. He refused to allow the deep wounds of a trusted friend to deter him from achieving God's purposes for his life.

Devotional focus:

I asked a student in the last few weeks of her freshman year to describe the struggles and difficulties she had faced. She told me that finding a true friend had been one of her biggest challenges. When she had first arrived at school, she had befriended several people, but during her second semester, she said, "Those who I thought were my friends turned out to be a lot different than they seemed." Another student, a junior, first met her suitemate and thought she was wonderful. Later, the suitemate proved to be both domineering and dictatorial, "laying down the law" about every aspect of their stay together. The freshman and the junior in these examples have both survived bad experiences. Though a little wounded, they have both gained valuable lessons. We can learn from close friends and from those whose actions or behavior disappoint us.

Students must never allow a broken friendship, or a betraying friendship, to hinder them. You can be loving, gentle, and kind in spite of how your friends treat you (Galatians 5:22-23). When a friendship turns sour, it need not sour you on friendship. The freshman above told me that she has now made new friends. She has moved beyond her disappointment, and she has made important adjustments in her journey toward completing her degree.

Journal reflection:

When the Melting Pot Boils

Scriptural insight:

And the contention was so sharp between them, that they departed asunder one from the other. (Acts 15:39)

The last story we expect to hear is one about Christians quarreling. We have all heard of churches and Christians arguing over various matters. For instance, they may differ over which person should lead a particular ministry or the method of selection used. Yet, disputes among Christians are more rare than some might lead you to believe. Christians live in harmony most of the time.

The last behavior I would have expected from such men as Paul and Barnabas was a quarrel so intense that they abruptly separated from each other. Luke tells us that a difference of opinion brought about this sharp contention. Barnabas wanted to give Mark a second opportunity at ministry; Paul opposed this choice.

Truth to tell, we all see things a little differently than others at times. Just look at any election for a picture of people with divergent views. Diversity must never destroy the unchangeable doctrines that we find in God's Word or cause us to lose control.

Paul eventually realized that he had been wrong about not giving Mark a second opportunity. Toward the end of his ministry, we see him acknowledging the value of the minister he had once opposed (2 Timothy 4:11). As a physical body heals from a cut, so the body of Christ heals through the soothing touch of the Holy Spirit.

Devotional focus:

College and university life could best be called "a melting pot" of people and ideas that must blend together to become a caring community. Look at these interesting but diverse examples as you consider such a community:

mature / childish	outgoing / shy	well adjusted / abused
wealthy / poor	popular / ignored	confident / unsure
focused / floundering	healthy / sickly	car / no car
capable / dependent	secure / anxious	talented / amateurish

articulate / bumbling   gifted / ordinary   beautiful / plain
obedient / rebellious   leaders / followers   sheltered / worldly wise
American / immigrant   serious / humorous   decisive / wavering
arrogant / humble   positive /negative   organized / scatterbrained
stable family life / changeable family life   private school / public school
transfer student / began as a freshmen   religious / secular
having family support / going it alone   unmarried / married / remarried

Many and varied roads have converged to bring you together with other students. Sometimes differences cause the melting pot to boil. Turf wars may occur over where to put belongings in a dorm room. One roommate may feel that he built the dorm and paid for it. Despite our distinctions, we must strive to be considerate of others. We must learn from their life experiences. We must refuse to be petty and easily offended over trivial matters. This may mean keeping your mouth shut sometimes. It may mean overlooking the faults and failures of those around you. It may mean giving ground in an argument. We must maintain our dignity while respecting others. When the pot boils, try turning down the heat!

Journal reflection:

Evaluating Your Friendships

Scriptural insight:

But Amnon had a friend, whose name was Jonadab. (2 Samuel 13:3)

For Amnon only is dead. (2 Samuel 13:33)

. . . one sinner destroyeth much good. (Ecclesiastes 9:18)

The rape of Tamar and the murder of Amnon make for a sordid, shocking story. Most families would try to cover up such a dark family secret and would certainly try to keep it out of print.

The story begins with a young man noticing a young lady. He has immoral thoughts toward her, which eventually leads to his destruction. Instead of asking for her hand in marriage, he chooses to seek immediate gratification. On the advice of a friend, he pretends to be sick so that Tamar will bring food to his bed and he can attack her. His plan works flawlessly. She comes with good intentions and food for Amnon. He suddenly grabs her and rapes her.

Let's not overlook a vital aspect of this terrible story. Amnon had a friend whose name was Jonadab. This friend had a special talent. He was good at scheming to help others get what they wanted. He was ready to get involved, and he was eager to offer his crafty advice. He could have written the book on manipulation. His devious scheme led to the death of his friend and the rape of Tamar, and it transformed Absalom into a fugitive. His influence had devastating effects upon King David's family, as Tamar, Amnon, and Absalom were all siblings. These terrible consequences all happened because Amnon had a foolish friend.

Devotional focus:

All adults should be able to evaluate and recognize the negative or positive influences within their lives. Children lack the ability or experience to recognize these pressures. When I was ten, my friend wanted to steal some watermelons. He advised me to slip out of the house after my parents fell asleep. His plan worked well, and we stole the delicious fruit on several occasions from a field a few blocks from home. No one ever caught us, but I returned years later and confessed, offering to pay for the melons. I regretted listening to my friend and participating in his plans. Living with mistakes can be hard, but rectifying mistakes can be rewarding.

A university sophomore told me she had to make new friends, because her old friends were back home. A college senior said, "The biggest problem I faced was finding friends that I could confide in." A university freshman, excited about attending school, chose the kind of friends he had known back home. He soon participated in the same destructive behavior. Before long, he left school in disgrace without achieving his vast potential.

We all need people on whom we can rely, but we must use great discretion in making new friends, always remembering to evaluate the influence of those who might hold that prized position. Have you prayed about finding new friends? Does the friendship challenge you to be a better person, to achieve your goals? Do you have the courage to refuse to participate in the person's harmful activities? If their influence is harmful, you may need new friends.

Journal reflection:

Conflict Resolution 101

Scriptural insight:

For it hath been declared unto me of you, my brethren, by them which are of the house of Chloe, that there are contentions among you. (1 Corinthians 1:11)

God's Word never attempts to conceal the occasional dissention, division, or conflict within the church. For example, Paul received word from Chloe that members of the Corinthian church were debating on which preacher they liked best. This, it turns out, proved to be just the tip of the iceberg. Later in Corinthians, Paul addresses numerous issues that had led to contention. He included a lot of thoughts within his letters to the Corinthians to resolve arguments.

Even Jesus' small group of twelve disciples squabbled. One disagreement erupted over how they should have sold a gift for money to help the poor (Matthew 26:8). Jesus commended the giver and chided the disciples. One story tells of the disciples' competition to see who was the greatest among them (Luke 22:24). In response to this discord, Jesus washed their feet to teach them about humility.

On many occasions in Scripture, we see that conflict can arise quickly and break the unity of any group. That is why so many Scriptural insights tell us about peace, longsuffering, unity, forgiveness, praying for our enemies, and love.

Devotional focus:

No matter how humble or peaceful you may be it seems that dissension will eventually find you, causing worry, stress, anxiety, loss of appetite, and sleepless nights. Some clashes arise because of serious matters. If a dorm resident possesses illegal substances and uses or distributes them, this will lead to serious conflict, as will a resident breaking other laws or physically abusing anyone. The college or university staff, the police, and the legal system must handle such serious issues.

The typical conflict within a dorm, however, erupts over trivial matters, with most prompted when one person disregards another's rights. Some may listen to a CD at 90 decibels all night or slam the door while you're sleeping. Others conveniently "borrow" your shampoo or toothpaste without permission. Still others may eat all the food you have just purchased. While these issues may seem minor, they can be exasperating and can lead to heated arguments.

Many books focus on conflict resolution, giving proven ways to handle clashes. Here is some homespun advice on dealing with these matters:

- When a dormitory resident offers criticism, think about it before responding. Some criticism can be positive; some, negative. Perhaps the resident's comments have merit.
- Do any of your actions violate the rights of others? Most students move into a dorm so they can live where the atmosphere is conducive to learning. A dorm is not a theme park or a vacation condominium. Students pay a lot of money for the privilege of living there and should be able to study and get a good night's sleep. Your rights cease where another person's rights begin.
- Are any of your actions motivated by a desire to strike back or get even? This only adds fuel to the fire and escalates the situation. Someone must be big enough to forgive and forget.
- Let trivial things go! If someone needs a little food, shampoo, toothpaste, or copy paper, then give it to them.
- Try to put the cause of the quarrel into a simple sentence. You'll be surprised at how that gives the issue the right perspective. "I'm mad because she used my shampoo." That doesn't sound like an earth-shattering infraction that should have caused you such stress.

This simple homespun advice can help you as you try to overcome conflict.

Journal reflection:

Chapter Five

Essentials for Classroom Success

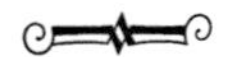

1. *Classroom Essentials*
2. *Remember to Study*
3. *Procrastination Consternation*
4. *Inspiration, Perspiration, and Motivation*
5. *What Do You Need to Succeed?*
6. *How To Become a Failure*
7. *The Easy Button*

Voices and Choices

"You must remember to show up for your classes."

"Get out of bed and go to class."

"Get your work done."

"Don't forget to study."

"Take a break from studying. It helps to get your mind off of it for a while. That helps you to regain your focus."

"Try to find a balance. Don't let bad things cause you to become negative about everything."

"I'm worried about getting distracted, self-discipline, and time management."

Journal Focus

List some ideas from the devotionals and from your new experiences in class about methods you need to adopt that will help you to succeed in class.

Strength Through Prayer

"Heavenly Father, I know that I need to succeed in the classroom if I am going to accomplish my goals. Please help me to stay focused and to be organized so that I can be successful. Amen."

Classroom Essentials

Scriptural insight:

Teach me good judgment and knowledge. (Psalm 119:66)

And it came to pass, that, as he was praying in a certain place, when he ceased, one of his disciples said unto him, Lord, teach us to pray, as John also taught his disciples. (Luke 11:1)

By some estimates, only about one percent of a billion people in underdeveloped nations ever have the opportunity to attend college. In America, tens of thousands of people either have no funds for college or find themselves trapped in a life situation that blocks them from attending school. Those trapped in a life situation learn from family, friends and experience. Those that have the privilege to attend a college must realize their great blessing and opportunity.

David never had the opportunity of attending school. Schooling for children in biblical times consisted of being taught at home. His parents had instilled within him a great desire to learn the Word of God, so he cried, "Teach me." The disciples heard Jesus communing with His father and asked Him to teach them to pray. These men revealed their eagerness to learn.

If your dreams are to become a reality so that you can achieve your goals and experience future success, one fact is certain: You must be teachable and desire knowledge.

Devotional focus:

It takes more than sitting in a classroom to gain success as a student. Practicing some classroom essentials, however, will help you to reach that goal:

- Get to know your professors and what they expect from you. You can make an instructor your adversary or your friend. Learn not only the professor's name, but also something about him. Does he have a family? Where did he attend school? Some may be open to friendship while others prefer to keep you at a distance. Either way, it never hurts to be sociable. You may need the help later that the professor has the power to provide.

- Listen during class lectures and learn to take good notes. Instructors often give hints about test materials, but you must be listening to catch them. You can think about your upcoming date later. In taking notes, learn to abbreviate some words to capture important points. Use a highlighter for emphasis. Learn to swap notes, compare notes, and copy notes in order to get all the class information you need.
- Avoid skipping class. Someone once said, "Half the battle is just showing up." Many of the students we interviewed advised: "Tell them to get out of bed and go to class." You can nap later. Go to class if you have a runny nose, if you have a headache, if someone has hurt your feelings. Practice discipline. Skipping can become a harmful habit.

Journal reflection:

Remember to Study

Scriptural insight:

Study to shew thyself approved unto God, a workman that needeth not to be ashamed. (2 Timothy 2:15)

A wise man will hear, and will increase learning; and a man of understanding shall attain unto wise counsels. (Proverbs 1:5)

My mouth shall speak of wisdom; and the meditation of my heart shall be of understanding. (Psalm 49:3)

Though we all need to remember many things, memorizing details and facts often proves challenging. I hate to admit it, but I have forgotten my home phone number more than once. With my cell phone programmed to speed dial for calling home, I have little need to remember it. At times, I have struggled to call to mind my Social Security number and my debit card PIN number. Remembering numerous passwords can also be challenging. Some of us have to admit that we have even forgotten where we parked while shopping at Wal-Mart.

However, our minds are amazing. Every day, we recall thousands of facts and details. Though the human brain weighs only about three pounds, it has more than a billion neuron cells capable of storing vast quantities of data. Biblical authors frequently remind us of the desirability of storing information. The Psalmist said, "Thy word have I hid in mine heart, that I might not sin against thee" (Psalm 119:11). How can we understand spiritual matters unless we're exposed to them? How can we be founded in the fundamentals of God's Word without reading and meditating upon it? Spiritual understanding comes only when we study and meditate upon the Bible.

Devotional focus:

To be a successful student, you must learn some lessons about learning some lessons. To make learning easier, first establish good study habits. We interviewed several students who said, "Don't forget to study." Educators will tell you to start preparing early for a test and then to refresh your memory with the details throughout the week. Pulling an all-nighter may occasionally be necessary, but it's best to start early. Second, join a good study group, which often gives a little extra incentive to learn. Finally, learn to use mnemonic devices. As you may know, the word "mnemonic" relates to memory aids. For instance, many students make up a poem or acronym that uses the letters of the information they need to recall. I once memorized the lobes of the brain using the words Front and TOP. On a test, I quickly wrote that the four lobes are frontal, temporal, occipital, and parietal.

How can you enhance your ability to study? Have you thought about your study habits? We hope these simple and brief observations will benefit you as you study.

Journal reflection:

___

___

___

___

___

___

___

___

___

___

___

___

Procrastination Consternation

Scriptural insight:

. . . and a wise man's heart discerneth both time and judgment. (Ecclesiastes 8:5)

Felix trembled, and answered, Go thy way for this time; when I have a convenient season, I will call for thee. (Acts 24:25)

Waiting, a precise course of action may have either positive or negative results. When we must make a hard decision, it often proves advantageous to wait and pray for direction. When we need rest, we may need to slow down, delaying all but essential tasks. Before we rush into signing our name and obligating ourselves to a loan, we need to take time to consider. On the other hand, waiting too long may prove ruinous, as when a farmer postpones planting a crop and never has a harvest to reap.

Putting off eternal matters for a more convenient time may also prove disastrous. We have no promise of more time or other opportunities. Felix was a man who chose to delay his decision about spiritual matters. The Bible shows no record of his making things right with God. Solomon advises us that a wise man can discern time and recognize the coming judgment. A wise person knows when to wait and when to take action.

Devotional focus:

You often see them at the mall, hanging out at a student center, or just walking around campus. I'm talking about students who seem to be wasting time. Some have time to kill, having just finished a paper or taken a test. They have earned a break, time to kick back. They often say, "I'm getting some down time." Other students, however, have a paper due the next day or a test early the next morning. They are trying to put off the inevitable. After wasting many valuable hours, they finally open a book or their notes to study, or they finally sit at a computer and try desperately to write that last-minute paper.

One student recently waited until the last possible moment to write nine project papers. She attempted to do this in one night. This kind of decision may get the adrenaline pumping, but it may also lead to submitting inferior papers. Waiting till the eleventh hour to memorize massive amounts of material can be a disaster. I've heard many students say, "I waited too late to study. I was too tired to learn the material. I flunked the test."

You can avoid procrastination consternation if you use time wisely. You can discipline yourself to prepare papers and memorize large amounts of data early. Then, before the test, you can look over your notes to refresh your memory. In making wise decisions about your time, you can often prevent exhaustion, frustration, stress, and anxiety. You'll be surprised how much better you feel when you get a good night's sleep before the test. Your higher test score might surprise you too.

Journal reflection:

Inspiration, Perspiration, and Motivation

Scriptural insight:

But charge Joshua, and encourage him, and strengthen him: for he shall go over before this people, and he shall cause them to inherit the land which thou shalt see. (Deuteronomy 3:28)

And David was greatly distressed . . . but David encouraged himself in the Lord his God. (1Samuel 30:6)

Joshua had been Moses' student for about 40 years. He had talked to Moses and listened to him. He had been prepared to take his teacher's place as the next leader of Israel. He had exhibited faith, courage, patience, and tenacity. He was both ready to take the helm and capable of far more than he realized. His time to lead had arrived.

Joshua may have felt intimidated at the prospect of following such an exceptional leader as Moses. He must have been deeply concerned about being accepted and about his ability to lead Israel. I believe that God saw his doubts and wanted to encourage him. God told Moses to share a personal word with Joshua. So Moses took time to speak to him, strengthening him.

I'm glad that God places just the right people around us to lift us up when we're down. At times, though, we are the ones who must take the initiative. For example, David encouraged himself through worship, something we too must do. Praying, reading the promises of God's Word, and singing also serve as great sources for spiritual inspiration.

Devotional focus:

Solomon, a man who had learned a lot about learning a lot, said, "... much study is a weariness of the flesh" (Ecclesiastes 12:12). Every student knows how exhausting studying can be. Someone once said, "Success is 10 percent inspiration and 90 percent perspiration." Preparing for a test, a paper, or a project takes a lot out of you. You may often hear a classmate say, "I have nothing left to give." After perspiration, we all need inspiration (and a shower).

How can we stay motivated to meet all the challenges and the many demands that we face?

- Surround yourself with people who inspire and motivate you.
- Get as much sleep and rest as possible to recharge your battery.
- Look at how far you have come and the many successes you've achieved already.
- Try a change of scenery, going somewhere peaceful and relaxing.
- Grab your ipod and listen to your favorite music.
- Go to a sports event or campus activity.
- Treat yourself to a big banana split, forgetting about the calories.
- Find some laughter somewhere.
- Take a long walk and revel in God's creation.

Joshua survived as the new leader of Israel. God took care of all his needs. Remember, He takes care of the sparrows, and He will take care of you. So take care of yourself and stay motivated.

Journal reflection:

____

____

____

____

____

____

____

What Do You Need to Succeed?

Scriptural insight:

If any of you lack wisdom, let him ask of God, that giveth to all men liberally, and upbraideth not; and it shall be given him. But let him ask in faith, nothing wavering. (James 1:5-6)

Many verses in the Bible let us know that God wants us to pray, and many verses show us how God responded when people did pray. Our Heavenly Father delights in answering prayers and meeting needs.

Jesus had a half brother named "James," whose epistle (letter), though brief, gives some basic information about living the Christian life. He shares special insight about trials, temptations, stability, and steadfastness, as well as ministry, partiality, faith, works, the tongue, strife, submission, patience, healing, and answered prayer.

When writing about prayer, he tells us how God responds, that He gives to us liberally, generously, and abundantly. He uses the words "upbraideth not" in his epistle. Our Heavenly Father meets our needs without scolding us for seeking Him. God encourages us to come to Him in prayer (Matthew 7:7-11).

God gives us His gifts because He is kind and merciful and because He loves us. His gifts meet our needs and help us to enjoy life. They make us whole and complete as we labor for Him (1Corinthians 12:7). In short, God answers many of our prayers to help us become successful.

Devotional focus:

Many people go shopping with an itemized list, one that has required time and thought to prepare. Every item has importance, so shoppers often go from store to store until they purchase every one.

I've seen dozens of high school students wandering various store aisles with a list of college needs. A complete list would require several pages, but, briefly, these lists include: summer and winter clothing, leisure and formal clothing, shoes, bathroom essentials, personal grooming provisions, bedding, furniture and accessories, kitchen appliances and cookware, cleaning supplies, sporting and musical equipment, a clock, a cell phone, a computer, and, of course, classroom materials. The underlying aim of all the purchases is to help students gain success.

Excelling as a student, however, depends upon more than the many items you bring with you. If you fail to be equally diligent about other goals, you will soon make drastic mistakes. Once you have organized your shopping list and room, you must organize your schedule. Get a desk calendar or student planner, and write down the meeting day and time for every class, reading assignments, and due dates for tests and research papers. These details will help to keep you on track.

What do you need to succeed? A good attitude, perseverance, and knowing what to do as you keep up with the many details on your schedule all serve as good examples.

Journal reflection:

How To Become a Failure

Scriptural insight:

And ye have forgotten the exhortation which speaketh unto you as unto children, My son, despise not thou the chastening of the Lord, nor faint when thou art rebuked of him: For whom the Lord loveth he chasteneth, and scourgeth every son whom he receiveth. If ye endure chastening, God dealeth with you as with sons; for what son is he whom the father chasteneth not? (Hebrews 12:5-7)

. . . reprove, rebuke, exhort with all longsuffering. (2 Timothy 4:2)

No one likes to take orders or to be disciplined. No one likes to be told they are wrong. We tend to draw back from those who hold us accountable. Words that correct us often anger and offend us. I would rather receive a compliment than criticism anytime. If correction, discipline, or advice wounds us, we may need to gain some maturity, so that we can hear the comments and decide whether they have any merit.

Correction and discipline serve valuable roles in society. A prosperous company has employees who heed their supervisors' instructions. A victorious army has soldiers who follow orders. A successful student learns to listen and follow directions.

If an instructor gives a student a failing grade or tells the student to rewrite a paper, there must be a reason. If he instructs a student to be in class or to be on time, it must be important.

A professor has a responsibility to the school to teach the student and to maintain an environment conducive to learning. A professor has a responsibility to the student to do his best to provide the most informative class possible.

The Bible talks about God rebuking and correcting us. It is part of the process of becoming a mature Christian. Paul reminded Timothy that he had the responsibility of correcting, rebuking, and encouraging.

So if a professor, pastor, employer, resident assistant, resident director, friend, or parent has a word of correction, please accept it without offense. They usually have your benefit and the benefit of others in mind. Taking correction to heart helps us achieve growth and maturity.

Devotional focus:

Let us give you some advice. This time, however, to illustrate a point, you have our permission to rebel and refuse to follow the destructive advice below. Let's toss out a few thoughts as we look at how to become a failure:

- You must bring some bad things with you from home. If you have grown up in dysfunction, hold on to it and refuse to become well adjusted. If you have been hurt, don't forgive or put any effort into being healed and whole.
- You need a bad attitude. Refuse to listen to those around you. Ignore their advice and do your own thing. Show them how stubborn, self-centered, rebellious, and opinionated you can be.
- You must disregard discipline. Stay up all night and sleep through your classes all day. Refuse to study or turn in assigned papers.
- Become distracted. Lose your focus and your direction.

Remember, we told you that this advice should be ignored. You have our permission to rebel and to disregard this advice. After all, you already knew that this advice was bad and harmful, didn't you?

Journal reflection:

The Easy Button*

Scriptural insight:

Behold, I am the Lord, the God of all flesh: is there any thing too hard for me? (Jeremiah 32:27)

. . . but knowledge is easy unto him that understandeth. (Proverbs 14:6)

Everyone knows that God can do anything. After all, Almighty God has omnipotent power. He even asked Jeremiah once if anything was too hard for Him, reminding Israel that He has all power and finds nothing too hard.

On the flip side, everyone knows that man finds many tasks too difficult. As finite, weak, and temporal creatures, our strength and existence depend upon the Lord. He has already brought us through thousands of life-threatening situations, His power proving sufficient and sustaining: "My grace is sufficient for thee: for my strength is made perfect in weakness" (2 Corinthians 12:9).

Scripture shows God's protective, enabling power: "There hath no temptation taken you but such as is common to man: but God is faithful, who will not suffer you to be tempted above that ye are able; but will with the temptation also make a way of escape, that ye may be able to bear it" (1 Corinthians 10:13).

Situations that handicap us, God finds easy. Our complex problems are simple for Him. He wants us to give Him our troubles; He has promised divine help and strength (Matthew 11:28-30).

Devotional focus:

The word "easy" has a multitude of definitions. See if you recognize any of these phrases: You made that look easy. He chose the easy way out. We have an easy payment plan. That book is an easy read. That comes easy to her. We're traveling to the Big Easy. It's quick and easy. That's easy listening. That's an easy recipe. Use Easy-Off spray. I want my eggs over easy. It's one easy step. She has an easy-bake oven. Easy does it. Take it easy. This is going to be easy.

Many students on college campuses across America know the word "easy." One chain store offers students an aid to help them in hard situations. Staples, with its "Easy Button," wants us to know that the company has made exchanging an empty ink cartridge or buying its products simple. Sales from the Easy Button have been so good that Staples donates a million dollars a year from its profits to Boys and Girls Clubs. When stressed students touch the button, a voice says, "That was easy." That voice, sure to give everyone a smile, aims to calm us down, reducing our stress.

We all wish the Easy Button really worked to fix all of life's hardships. Alas, for these problems, it has the power to make us smile, perhaps laugh, and nothing more. Solomon told us that knowledge comes easy to the person who understands. Applying oneself certainly helps to make things easier. Actually, the plan for making things easy is, in fact, easy:

- Do reading assignments and highlight important material.
- Outline important points and information that you will need.
- Take time to review material throughout the week.
- Avoid cramming for every test. Try to memorize material during the week.
- Start to work early on papers and projects.

Have you ever left a test and thought that it seemed easier than you expected? Why did you think that? Did you approach the test differently? Can you think of other ways to make life easier? Try to work consistently, and . . . take it easy.

*Adapted from Staples advertising campaign.

Journal reflection:

Chapter Six

Formulating a Positive Attitude

1. *What Is Right With Your School?*
2. *The Code of Conduct*
3. *An Educator's Heart*
4. *The Supporting Cast*
5. *Recognizing the Sacrifices of Others*
6. *Proactive About Your Progress*
7. *Step in Time*

Voices and Choices

"Practice structure and discipline."

"The culture shock was the hardest thing. I am from the north and things are a little different there. I'm doing better now."

"I grew up in an orphanage. I could blame others for the pain that I've known in the past. I don't know why some of the kids I've taught want to continue to blame others. You don't have to continually blame others for your difficulties."

"I was very nervous before I went to orientation. That calmed me down. Our university has many clubs and organizations. I want to get involved."

"I had to work at learning time management."

Journal Focus

How many positive things have you noticed about your school? If you have overlooked the good things that have been provided for you, reflect upon some of them and make a list in your journal.

Strength Through Prayer

"Lord, it is so easy to fall into a rut of feeling negative about everything. Help me to recognize the many sacrifices of others that make my education a possibility. Help me to learn to be thankful for my opportunities and blessings. Amen."

What Is Right With Your School?

Scriptural insight:

Well done, good and faithful servant. (Matthew 25:23)

Notwithstanding ye have well done, that ye did communicate with my affliction. (Philippians 4:14)

The Bible may speak of dissension and contention within the early church, but it also speaks of harmony and progress among these new Christians. Within God's Word, we find both notable hindrances and remarkable heroes, both the faithful and the unfaithful.

In a parable (Matthew 25:14-30), Jesus condemned the unprofitable servant, yet He praised the faithful servants with the words, "Well done." Paul had to deal with deserters and dissension within the fledgling church, but he had words of commendation for those who helped him.

The Bible firmly condemns the unfaithful, and it firmly applauds the faithful. The attitude and actions of various people in the Bible determined their reward. It shows a positive mindset as a great determining factor in a successful and rewarding future.

Devotional focus:

The meeting consisted of church leaders. All had ample opportunity to address any pertinent issues, as the chairman went from one person to the next and asked simply, "Tell me, what is right about our church? What are some of the good things that we are accomplishing?" When the question made its way to a particularly critical leader, he refused to answer and said simply, "I pass." The church had had many great successes, yet he could offer nothing positive to say. Though his family had received much help, he remained silent. That incident and that individual point to the reality of a negative mindset. A similar story could well be told of many conversations in schools throughout America. I've listened to students speak negatively about every aspect of their college experience. If you ask them to tell you about their school, you'll hear about the bad food, bad professors, and terrible dorm life.

If someone asked you what's right with your school, would you have trouble discerning and sharing the many benefits of your school? For instance:

- Can you get hot meals with a wide selection of food?
- Do you have an air-conditioned and heated dorm room?
- Have you received any financial help?
- Have you made any friends?
- Will your education open up career doors of opportunity?
- Do the administration and faculty listen when you have a problem?
- Does the school offer activities for your enjoyment?
- Do you think they really care about you?
- Have others sacrificed to make your education possible?

I hope you can see some good things about your school. An optimistic mindset plays an essential role in your education. Try to mention some positive things about your school the next time someone asks you about it. Try to get away from all the negative thinking.

Journal reflection:

The Code of Conduct

Scriptural insight:

I will behave myself wisely in a perfect way. (Psalm 101:2)
[Love] doth not behave itself unseemly. (1 Corinthians 13:5)
. . . that they be in behaviour as becometh holiness. (Titus 2:3)
. . . vigilant, sober, of good behaviour. (1 Timothy 3:2)

We have all heard of teachers and counselors who have had to schedule appointments to discuss a child's bad behavior in school. You may have been on either side of this problem. In such situations, parents usually assume a defensive posture. After all, the problem must stem from the teacher or another student.

A second grade teacher once told a misbehaving child, "I've taken two minutes from the class to handle those who are misbehaving. You have robbed the other 30 children of two minutes of their time. If you multiply two minutes by 30 students, you discover that you have taken 60 minutes of instructional time from us." That comment made an impression upon a young mind.

The Bible tells us that we should behave wisely. Fun and humor do have their place. In fact, most students in classrooms enjoy lots of laughter. Those who misbehave in class, on campus, and in life, however, often hurt themselves and others. Misbehaving may sound like a childhood problem. Ask any teacher, however, about misbehavior, and he will tell you that higher education suffers greatly from bad and destructive behavior.

Devotional focus:

Many schools require students to read a code of conduct handbook that outlines the behavior the school expects from them on campus. The military and many companies have similar rules. Often, the reader must sign a statement showing that he has read the book and will abide by the regulations. Why does a school need rules, boundaries, and standards? Without proper behavior, the educational environment would disintegrate, giving students an inferior education and making them ill prepared for their profession. One freshman, told repeatedly to keep the school curfew and reminded that the curfew served as protection, chose to ignore the many warnings. One night, I saw the student returning from an after-curfew expedition and learned that the student had been raped and was almost killed.

Frankly, I've seen many students forfeit an educational opportunity, simply because they chose to circumvent the rules. Some seemed to thrive on living on the edge and flirting with disciplinary action. Professors and administrators will survive these encounters, though they may secretly wonder why the student chooses such destructive behavior and seems so casual about preparing for his future. This devotional may seem offensive; however, your development, success, and perhaps even your life may hinge upon how well you keep your agreement to abide by the code of conduct. Have you signed a covenant with your school? Why do you think the school needs a code of conduct? Are you doing your best to keep your promises?

Journal reflection:

____

____

____

____

____

____

____

____

____

An Educator's Heart

Scriptural insight:

Do we begin again to commend ourselves? Or need we, as some others, epistles of commendation to you, or letters of commendation from you? Ye are our epistle written in our hearts, known and read of all men: Forasmuch as ye are manifestly declared to be the epistle of Christ ministered by us, written not with ink, but with the Spirit of the living God; not in tables of stone, but in fleshly tables of the heart. (2 Corinthians 3:1-3)

Sooner or later, most of us will need letters of reference for an educational opportunity or a job that we want to pursue. Those in charge of the new prospect may ask for the name of friends, so they can call and ask questions about us. Quite often, we'll need to submit reference letters along with our resume. These friends know us. They know our character and potential. We expect them to represent us in the best possible light.

Paul talked to the Corinthians about letters of recommendation. He reminded them that they knew him, and he required no reintroduction to them. Nor did he need to find someone to write a letter to represent him. He pointed them to their hearts, which would reveal many memories. Most simply, their hearts offered verification of his love for them.

Devotional focus:

Students rarely have an opportunity to rub shoulders with educators or to get to know them in a personal way. Most students exchange pleasantries in the classroom and listen to a teacher's lectures for a semester or quarter and never really get to know them. Wouldn't it be interesting to ask your teachers some questions? For instance, why did they choose the field of education? Where did they go to school? What was their most difficult challenge in pursuing a degree? What sacrifices did they make to become teachers? Let me give you answers to some of these questions. Most teachers and administrators chose their careers, many at an early age, because they wanted to help others learn. They want you to be successful. Many of them could have walked an easier road and made more money. They have made great sacrifices to become teachers or administrators.

As Paul needed no letter of commendation, neither do educators need one. In tirelessly giving themselves to students, they reveal their hearts' desires. I've talked privately with some educators. You may never know how your accomplishments fill them with excitement and satisfaction. If you have the opportunity to ask your educators some questions, by all means take advantage of it. If not, you can still be certain of their dedication, because they have chosen to help you.

Journal reflection:

The Supporting Cast

Scriptural insight:

And it came to pass, when Moses held up his hand, that Israel prevailed: and when he let down his hand, Amalek prevailed. But Moses' hands were heavy; and they took a stone, and put it under him, and he sat thereon; and Aaron and Hur stayed up his hands, the one on the one side, and the other on the other side; and his hands were steady until the going down of the sun. (Exodus 17:11-12)

The Bible gives us some of the details about the battle between Israel and Amalek. Israel had divine promises from God that the Lord would go before its people. God promised certain victory, but Israel still had to fight. On this particular occasion, Israel remained victorious as long as Moses kept his hands lifted up. When he let his hands drop, the enemy began to prevail. The mysterious circumstances of this battle must certainly have some lessons for us. Did God want future generations to recognize the value of praise? We, in fact, have a scriptural mandate to lift our hands in worship. Did God want us to see that He provides the strength that makes a Christian victorious? Did He mean to show us that we need the support of others in spiritual warfare? I believe this story illustrates all of these lessons.

The hands of Moses grew weary. I can picture his muscles beginning to twitch as he tried to endure. He saw the consequences of letting his hands down. Aaron and Hur recognized that Moses needed help. They put a rock under him, and both supported his hands lifted toward heaven. This team effort brought God's help and victory for Israel. Throughout the Bible we see people struggling to survive. Then, we often see other believers gathering alongside to give assistance and support.

Devotional focus:

One cell phone company runs a powerful television commercial. It shows hundreds of people standing behind the person who uses that service. The company wants you to know that you will have lots of support, if you sign up with them. Let's look at some other examples of support. My wife and I noticed the credits at the end of a movie the other night. We found amazing the hundreds of people it took to make this one movie. It also surprised me to discover that Lance Armstrong had a large entourage supporting him as he won numerous Tour de France races. Churches remain open and missionaries continue to serve because of support.

Another example occurs at a graduation exercise. The university or college staff dresses in school colors and marches in together. Its members uphold you and make your education possible, yet students rarely think about this support. The government provides grants and loans. Schools furnish scholarships. People or corporations fund endowments for scholarships. Students usually arrive on campus wearing clothes, driving a car, and carrying boxes of supplies and appliances. Somehow, someone pays their tuition and buys their books. Parents often sacrifice their own desires, because they love their kids and want to support their education. If you ever feel as though you're going it alone, remember that not only does the school support you, but so does a large group of family and friends.

Journal reflection:

____

____

____

____

____

____

____

____

Recognizing the Sacrifices of Others

Scriptural insight:

Whereunto I am appointed a preacher, and an apostle, and a teacher of the Gentiles. For the which cause I also suffer these things. (2 Timothy 1:11-12)

For I bear him record, that he hath a great zeal for you. (Colossians 4:13)

No one ever means to appear thoughtless concerning blessings, gifts, or privileges. At times, we acknowledge with great care and gratitude a gift that we need and enjoy. Yet, we fail to offer thanks for other gifts, because we become preoccupied with the minutiae of daily living and schedules crammed with activities and responsibilities.

Paul occasionally reminded some of the early churches of blessings they enjoyed due to sacrifices others had made to spread the gospel and establish the church. He said, "For all things are for your sakes, that the abundant grace might through the thanksgiving of many redound to the glory of God" (2 Corinthians 4:15). Another time, he detailed some of the sufferings he had endured for the cause of Christ and to launch the church (2 Corinthians 11:24-28). He wanted them to be aware of the sacrifices of others and to show appreciation.

Devotional focus:

Most students never give a single thought to the countless sacrifices others have made so they can pursue an education. Students attend a school that was once the dream of someone who saw the need and benefit of education. The visionary, who dreamed of birthing the college or university, had to find the people who would finance his dream to the tune of millions of dollars. He found engineers to design the campus and carpenters, electricians, plumbers, painters, and others to complete the physical plant, including the dorms and parking lots. Then, he hired professors and purchased equipment to enhance the students' learning experience. Over the years, staff helped set up endowments and scholarships. Through the whole process, countless donors made great financial sacrifice, giving funds they might have spent elsewhere. Few students think about the tremendous amount of money necessary to pay the staff and maintain the institution. I wish I had thought about these things years ago. I believe I would have been more grateful. It's not too late to say thank you to the many people who work and sacrifice to keep the dream alive. On behalf of the alumni, we offer a heartfelt thank you. On behalf of current students, let the administrators and staff know that you sincerely appreciate all the sacrifices they are making.

Journal reflection:

Proactive About Your Progress

Scriptural insight:

Epaphras, who is one of you, a servant of Christ, saluteth you, always labouring fervently for you in prayers, that ye may stand perfect and complete in all the will of God. (Colossians 4:12)

That the man of God may be perfect, thoroughly furnished unto all good works. (2 Timothy 3:17)

Some New Testament writers frequently stated primary objectives for laboring among the churches. They addressed areas of growth, maturity, and talent, as well as labor for Christ. Paul talked about seeing believers conformed to the image of Christ (Romans 8:29), and about all members in the body applying themselves and working together (Ephesians 4:16). He wanted them to understand that they labored with Christ to reap a harvest (1 Corinthians 3:9).

The apostles expected great things of the early church. Their writings often chided, corrected, mentored, rebuked, and challenged believers to strive to meet these expectations. They knew the potential of these first Christians, so they seemed to push—and push hard—to propel them toward growth and maturity. I'm sure that many in the early church whined about the apostles' leadership methods. In the end, however, the church would have a group of mature believers, capable of doing good works. They would be complete in the will of God and be able to take a stand as they performed their duty.

Devotional focus:

None of us like to be pushed; nor do we appreciate being told what to do or how to do it. We find ourselves in this situation when we enter school. The pushing begins in the first class when the professor hands us a syllabus that states attendance expectations; assigns papers, projects, and tests; and describes other course requirements. As we go over the syllabus in class, we often hear groans and see frowns. Let's face it—we would rather avoid hard work. Given the opportunity, we will choose the easiest path every time. Many students fail to realize that the state mandates the materials to be covered, and the administration assigns objectives. In addition, leaders have carefully reviewed the course to determine areas that must be included so students will fully understand the subject. The school must be proactive about your progress.

What stands as the number one objective of a school? Why do teachers often push so hard? Why must subjects be so difficult? The answers lie in understanding what motivates these teachers and administrators. Their number one objective: to make you successful in your chosen career. Contrary to what many may think, college precedes a career, and the courses you take help to make you marketable in a competitive world. A position will usually go to the person deemed most capable. I certainly want a skilled doctor examining me, a proficient auto technician fixing my brakes, and a knowledgeable teacher instructing me.

When the professor pushes and you feel the pressure, please remember: School officials want to prepare you, to help you to be successful, and to make you marketable. If you want to be capable and knowledgeable in your career, then you must accept some pushing.

Journal reflection:

____

____

____

____

____

____

____

____

Step in Time

Scriptural insight:

For we hear that there are some which walk among you disorderly. (2 Thessalonians 3:11)

Paul talked about some Christians whose walk had been out of order, causing the church at Thessalonica to experience problems. Paul had already told them "how they ought to walk" (1 Thessalonians 4:1), in a spiritual manner that would please the Lord. His letters stepped on some toes as he attempted to get them back in step. All of us should want to keep in step with other Christians. As soldiers in the army of the Lord, we must stay unified as we march together to serve our Commander. We must avoid getting out of step and causing our fellow soldiers to stumble. We know that we march with tall ones and short ones in this army of the Lord, so we must do our best to stay in time despite our differences. The next time a leader steps on your toes, remember that he wants to help you get back in step.

Devotional focus:

A veteran, talking about the art of marching, explained the intricate way that military units march in rank. I listened with interest as he shared from his vast experience and knowledge. He said that soldiers step off with their left foot when they march in rank. Starting out with the left foot can be challenging for right-handed people, but they must learn and use this rule. This veteran discussed the challenge of marching with soldiers of different body frames. Some taller soldiers may have to shorten their steps, while some shorter soldiers may have to increase theirs. One soldier getting out of step can throw off the pace of the whole unit. When a soldier gets out of step, the soldier behind him will automatically step on his heel. Sometimes a soldier will purposely step on an out-of-time marcher. The little pressure on the heel says, "Step in time!" When units have to run in formation, they absolutely must step in time. Soldiers could choose to exercise their freedom and march the way they desire, but this would lead to disaster, and the drill sergeant would quickly give them a few choice words.

Students, too, have a lot of choices. Freshmen often experience freedom for the first time when they leave home and go away to school. No one tells them when to go to bed or reminds them of tasks they should do. No one closely monitors their actions to keep them on the right path. This newfound independence proves more than some can handle. They soon walk in paths that shock their friends. Poor choices and actions push them out of step.

Years ago, I heard about a young man who decided to step beyond the warning signs and over the fence that kept him from the edge of a cliff. He shocked a crowd of onlookers as he moved closer to the edge in an attempt to entertain them. He failed to notice the gradual decline until it was too late, and he fell to his death. Living on the edge may seem exciting and elicit lots of attention, but the consequences often prove devastating. A student forced to leave school because of disciplinary action may find it painful. Even more painful, he will be powerless to go back and do it over, avoiding his mistakes. So remember, if someone steps on your heel or toe in offering advice or constructive criticism, take it to heart and get back in step.

Journal reflection:

____

____

____

____

____

____

____

Chapter Seven

Discovering Your Potential

1. *Pardon Me for Staring*
2. *The Underdog Story*
3. *Campus Construction*
4. *Beyond Your Wildest Dreams*
5. *The Darkroom*
6. *Don't Talk to Me Like That*
7. *Discovering Your Gifts in the Most Unlikely Places*

Voices and Choices

"Get out of your comfort zone."

"I am from outside of the USA. Mom was crying and I was crying when I left home. I came here all by myself. I didn't know where to go or what to do. I had no help, no car, and no friends. I prayed a lot. I had to calm myself down. I began to make some friends. They stood with me and helped me. I'm doing just fine now."

"I've learned that some of those who don't seem to have great potential as students can also accomplish great things."

"I didn't think I could make it as a college student. I worked hard, applied myself, and I accomplished more than I ever thought possible."

Journal Focus

Are you guilty of focusing too much on your weaknesses and on your obstacles? This week focus on your strengths and journal some thoughts about your assets and abilities.

Strength Through Prayer

"Father, at times we all question our ability and search for strength and confidence. Please help me look at my strengths and not my weaknesses. Help me to discover my potential and my purpose. Amen."

Pardon Me for Staring

Scriptural insight:

And Jesus, walking by the sea of Galilee, saw two brethren, Simon called Peter, and Andrew his brother, casting a net into the sea: for they were fishers. And he saith unto them, Follow me, and I will make you fishers of men. And they straightway left their nets, and followed him. And going on from thence, he saw other two brethren, James the son of Zebedee, and John his brother, in a ship with Zebedee their father, mending their nets; and he called them. And they immediately left the ship and their father, and followed him. (Matthew 4:18-22)

People like to watch others fish. Some weekly television programs on fishing draw many viewers. Anglers watch to pick up new fishing techniques. Others, too busy to go fishing, watch with bated breath and dream of having time to wet a hook. Before long, all the viewers wish to sit in a boat with a rod or to wade in the river fishing.

Jesus stood on the shore of the Sea of Galilee and watched several fishermen as they plied their trade—Simon and Andrew casting their net, James and John mending theirs. Jesus, however, had no interest in learning to fish. Rather, He gazed at these men for another reason: He saw their potential as disciples. Then, Jesus looked at Simon and Andrew and invited them to follow Him, referring to their occupation in His invitation: "I will make you fishers of men." All four men made the decision to follow Jesus.

Devotional focus:

You may gaze at a sunrise, a sunset, a mountain, or the sea and find it relaxing, but our society considers a person who looks intently at another to be rude. I confess I have a habit of staring, usually when I'm on a college campus or at a youth gathering. The subject of my gaze need do nothing weird or amazing to capture my attention. Rather, I stare at any gathering of young people because I see immense potential in them. Pardon me if I seem to be staring. I am thinking of the budding teachers, lawyers, doctors, ministers, businessmen, and musicians standing before me. I see the talent they possess to influence others. I wonder what grand accomplishments their future holds. I reflect on the growth process that may transform them into amazing leaders.

Many stare into a mirror and see themselves as failures or, at the least, as lacking talent, but I see a different image. Rather than focusing on your hair color, pimples, or your freckles, I observe your enormous potential. So, if you catch me staring at you, please indulge me. I'm just imagining the exciting and valuable future that lies ahead of you.

Journal reflection:

The Underdog Story

Scriptural insight:

And Samuel said unto Jesse, Are here all thy children? And he said, There remaineth yet the youngest, and, behold, he keepeth the sheep. And Samuel said unto Jesse, Send and fetch him: for we will not sit down till he come hither. And he sent, and brought him in. Now he was ruddy, and withal of a beautiful countenance, and goodly to look to. And the Lord said, Arise, anoint him: for this is he. (1 Samuel 16:11-12)

Samuel arrived at Jesse's home on a mission. The Lord had sent him to anoint a new king after He had rejected King Saul for disobedience. Samuel watched and awaited the Lord's direction as seven of Jesse's sons passed before him. The procession started with Eliab. This son looked like a potential king (1 Samuel 16:6), however, God told Samuel to disregard Eliab's countenance and stature. The Lord told Samuel that, unlike people who look at the outward appearance, He looks at a person's heart (1 Samuel 16:7). These seven sons may have all looked like prospective kings, but the Lord withheld His direction to anoint any of them. When Samuel asked Jesse if he had any other sons, he responded that the youngest was tending the sheep, and then, at Samuel's request, sent for David. As soon as David arrived, the Lord told Samuel to anoint him.

Now, I may be reading between the lines a little and making some assumptions, but I like to think that David was smaller than his siblings and that his family looked down on him due to his age. He may have seemed the least likely candidate for the position. Others may have questioned what God saw in this young man. Even David may have questioned his potential, but eventually he recognized his God-given ability to lead.

Devotional focus:

Growing up, I watched many different cartoons on television every Saturday morning. One cartoon featured a superhero canine dog. His shoeshine job served as his cover. Should sweet Polly Purebred get into trouble, he would dash to the rescue and speak his reassuring motto, "There's no need to fear, Underdog is here!" If someone saw him flying to the rescue, they would usually hear him say, "Not bird, nor plane, nor even frog, it's just little ol' me, Underdog!" The most unlikely looking superhero of all time, he would never inspire hope or confidence. Even so, at the end of an episode, Underdog stood victorious despite his looks.

We read of some Bible heroes like Underdog. Moses may have stuttered, but he pastored the largest church of all time. Gideon may have been shy, but God used him to bring a mighty victory for Israel. David may have been small, but he felled a giant. Frequently, I've witnessed people considered to be underdogs who have accomplished amazing victories. Their test scores may have been average, but they usually had tenacity. They may have stammered a bit when standing before a group but have shown hidden strength. They may have turned in a mediocre project paper but then written a best seller. They may have appeared to have little aptitude, but their determination has made up for it. They may have been poor before but own a large company now.

History verifies that underdogs often become overachievers. People thought Abraham Lincoln a loser, but he became president. They considered Albert Einstein a failure, but he became one of the greatest intellectuals of all time. Ignore those who treat you as a failure or who assume you can accomplish nothing. Believe in yourself. You can graduate from college and become successful.

Journal reflection:

____

____

____

____

____

Campus Construction

Scriptural insight:

Ye also, as lively stones, are built up a spiritual house. (1 Peter 2:5)

The Bible refers to Christians in many ways. For instance, it calls us sheep, a bride, branches, light, and salt. Christians, however, often overlook the analogy that likens us to building materials, such as lumber, bricks, nails, drywall, pipes, shingles, carpet, and glass. Men and women, boys and girls from around the world make up the materials necessary to build the church. Peter compared us to living stones that have been placed in a spiritual house. Even within the United States, the kingdom of God has broad diversity, yet we have unity within the body of Christ (Ephesians 4:16). The blood of Jesus that has saved us (1 Peter 1:18-19) makes us sons of God, and part of the family of God (1 John 3:1-2). We can all expect to reach the same eternal destination (John 14:2-3).

Devotional focus:

Over the years, we have driven across many college campuses and have observed their constant construction projects. They must build new structures to keep pace with increasing enrollment or must refurbish existing buildings. Any new construction begins as a dream. Then, the school hires engineers to design it, prepare the ground, order materials, and turn it into a reality. Yet, the supreme construction project on any campus requires no cement, steel, or lumber. Rather, it lies in building students. Young people envision what they can become. They work hard with a school staff that labors to help them accomplish their hopes. Finally, with diploma in hand, they realize their dream.

Building projects of all sorts may teach us important lessons. If you ever find yourself in the Washington, D.C. area, try to visit one particular church. About a million visitors a year make a point to see the beautiful Washington National Cathedral. Construction began in 1907 and ended 83 years later in 1990. Its foundation stones came from Jerusalem; its 63 giant bells, from England. A small piece of moon rock, a gift from President Nixon, became part of a window. The cathedral staff employed some of the world's top craftsmen and used some of the world's finest building materials. A few years ago, our church had a remodeling project. The carpenter examined the quality of the boards and other materials. He accepted the best, but rejected some supplies, saying, "These materials will not do!" Church buildings are built from the best materials.

I'm thankful for the Lord's role as a Master Builder. He gave Noah a precise plan for the ark and Moses an exact design for the tabernacle. Master builders usually refuse all but the best supplies for their projects. God, on the other hand, has often chosen the poorest quality materials to build His structures. The Bible tells us, "He is able also to save them to the uttermost that come unto God by him" (Hebrews 7:25). Take a look at the materials that Jesus chose to build with:

- Mary Magdalene was possessed with seven devils (Luke 8).
- Zacchaeus was an embezzler (Luke 19).
- The lunatic of Gadara was possessed with a legion of demons (Mark 5).
- The woman at the well had been divorced five times (John 4).
- A lame man had waited 38 years for a miracle (John 5).
- A murderer turned into a missionary (Acts 9).

I've heard similar stories from some of my church members and friends, who have shared their past with me.

- "Pastor, I was an alcoholic for 21 years, but the Lord saved me."
- "Pastor, I was a harlot, but the Lord saved me."
- "Pastor, I was a drug dealer. I flushed $5,000 worth of marijuana down the toilet when the Lord saved me."
- "Preacher, I murdered two men, but the Lord saved me."

I'm so thankful that God chooses building materials that others reject. He takes anyone willing to accept Him as the Saviour. His skillful hands fashion us to become part of His beautiful church. He is actively working in us to build us spiritually and educationally.

Journal reflection:

Beyond Your Wildest Dreams

Scriptural insight:

And Joseph dreamed a dream, and he told it his brethren. (Genesis 37:5)

. . . we shall see what will become of his dreams. (Genesis 37:20)

The story of Joseph stands as one of the most exciting stories in the Bible. While a teenager, he suddenly began to have dreams. Perhaps he never fully understood the implication of his dreams, but his brothers certainly did. To them, his dreams meant that Joseph would be elevated above them, and that they would be his servants. We see envy, hate, deception, betrayal, slavery, temptation, and jail time as part of this exciting story, which reveals how God brought the dreams to pass. Eventually, we see Joseph's promotion, a tearful reunion, and a unified family. It makes me smile when I read about his brothers bowing before him, as his dream actually became a reality.

Those who dream often face difficulty. Others may be skeptical or critical, and may even oppose a person who dreams. Often, the opinion of others and facing difficulties rob people of their dreams. The life of Joseph teaches valuable lessons about achieving dreams. He persevered in spite of being misunderstood and mistreated. He endured in spite of being falsely accused and unjustly imprisoned. Dreams rarely come to pass overnight. Joseph had to wait several years before he rode in a royal chariot, wore royal apparel, sat upon a throne, and witnessed his family bowing before him. He was, no doubt, filled with the knowledge that God does make dreams come true.

Devotional focus:

Studies have revealed that a college education has many wonderful benefits, giving knowledge and expertise, opening doors of opportunity, and providing a good standard of living and success. My dream of receiving an education and achieving valuable accomplishments came when I made friends with a college graduate.

Witnessing what a good education had meant to him inspired me to pursue that goal.

Both my parents had dropped out of school to help support their families. No one in my family had ever received a college degree. So when I voiced my dream of attending school, people expressed skepticism. As I made my way through school, I stood alone, with little financial or verbal support. I persevered, however, and graduation immediately opened doors of opportunity for me. My degree rewarded me with success and fulfillment. My education propelled my life beyond my wildest dreams. Other graduates want you to know that you, too, may expect this reality. Their success and accomplishments have surpassed all their expectations. They encourage you to believe that dreams can come true. You, too, may surpass your expectations. Your voice can be added to the long list of alumni who readily say, "My education has taken me beyond my wildest dreams."

Journal reflection:

The Darkroom

Scriptural insight:

He hath set me in dark places. (Lamentations 3:6)
For now we see through a glass darkly. (1Corinthians 13:12)

Few people may want to read a book about tears. Yet, the Old Testament book of Lamentations could best be described as a volume concerning tears. Its core figure, Jeremiah the prophet, wept for the children of Israel. He relates his pain and talks about his tears. Jeremiah acknowledged that God had allowed him to go through some painful situations. The people beat and imprisoned him for being a true prophet (Jeremiah 20:1-3). They lowered him into an old miry well, where he sank down (Jeremiah 38:6). He felt his circumstances pulling him in pieces (Lamentations 3:11). He felt darkness surrounding him, and he knew neither when nor if he would get out.

Paul also referred to darkness when he talked about our present journey through this world. "Darkness" refers to spiritual wickedness (Ephesians 6:12), and relates to a lack of knowledge and understanding (Ephesians 4:18). This word also refers to being in a difficult place with no clue of which way to go (Psalm 18:28).

Psalms describes Israel as being in a dark place and needing to be delivered (Psalm 107:10, 14). This psalm tells us that God brought His people out of darkness and gave them freedom, but the process came neither instantly nor speedily. They experienced about 400 more years of darkness in Egypt before God sent deliverance. They later experienced 70 years of captivity before the light of deliverance came. Sometimes, we must wait a long time for a spiritual sunrise.

Devotional focus:

We still have an old Polaroid One Step camera at our house. These cameras, forerunners of the new digital camera technology, will soon be relics. In fact, most students have never seen a Polaroid One Step. This camera, once the most advanced camera on the market, allowed you simply to point, shoot the picture, pull out the developing film, and wait for the picture to develop. It took only a few minutes to develop a picture, but impatient photographers thought it seemed like an hour. The dark shadows slowly took shape, and the picture would slowly develop right before your eyes. Even further back, the instamatic camera used a roll of film that you dropped off at a developing location. The technician would place the film in chemicals in a darkroom and slowly develop the pictures, making negatives. Then he would use these to print your photographs. This method took a lot of time.

These images came to my mind as I thought about students waiting patiently for their future to develop. They often feel the obscurity of their lives, as though they're in a darkroom. Then, they must wait to see a picture developing. Finally, patient students realize that they have escaped the darkroom and that their lives are finally and fully developed.

Journal reflection:

Don't Talk to Me Like That

Scriptural insight:

A voice of noise from the city, a voice from the temple, a voice of the Lord that rendereth recompence to his enemies. (Isaiah 66:6)

There are, it may be, so many kinds of voices in the world. (1 Corinthians 14:10)

God has blessed most of us with the ability to share our thoughts and emotions through speech. Some voices ring high like a soprano, while others are low like a baritone. Some voices flow out soft and mellow, while others thunder out loud and harsh. The way we use our voices can bless others or wound them. The Bible talks of many different kinds of voices.

Often referring to influence, a voice may come from the "city" (Isaiah 66:6), and sway us toward evil, from the "temple" and persuade us to do good, or from "the Lord" and send us along Godly paths. We may use our vocal cords to teach, sing, preach, pray, witness, and encourage, or we may employ them to judge, criticize, condemn, curse, discourage, threaten, and destroy. We choose how we use our voices.

Words carry tremendous power. Spoken in haste, they may be hurtful; uttered in love, they often encourage. Words can hang over us for a lifetime. For instance, many of us can quote verbatim famous words of political leaders. That's why it's important to think before you speak, weighing your words carefully. Sometimes you may even have to hold your tongue. How are you using your gift of speech to influence others? How are the voices that surround you influencing you?

Devotional focus:

Working on this book has allowed us to talk with lots of people. I doubt that we will ever forget some of the exchanges we've had as we've interviewed students from various walks of life, from various schools, and at different stages on their educational journey. We also welcomed the insight we gained in conversations with teachers, professors, businessmen, and administrators.

Especially surprising and inspiring was a conversation we had with one doctor who showed how a person can rise above difficulty to become successful anyway. World renown in many respects and circles, this successful doctor has published several books. He informed me that some of his high school teachers talked down to him, telling him he would fail. Few saw his potential and many even called him a failure. With their words and expectations of him forever imprinted upon his mind, he said he fully expected to fail and entered college with that outlook. He did fail the first test during his first semester, and he promptly wrote a sad letter home to tell his family that he would probably have to drop out of college. As the semester progressed, however, he turned his failure into success, surprising himself and everyone else by making the dean's list. Now, 40 years later, he still remembers those discouraging words. His life stands as a shining example that has proven them wrong, because he rose above the negative voices and the destructive influences. His life inspires me and motivates me to say something to all those who talk down to students with a dream. If you must talk down to students and tell them they will fail, then perhaps the students will have something to say to you: "Don't talk to me like that!"

Journal reflection:

Discovering Your Gifts in the Most Unlikely Places

Scriptural insight:

For as we have many members in one body, and all members have not the same office: So we, being many, are one body in Christ, and every one members one of another. Having then gifts differing according to the grace that is given to us, whether prophecy, let us prophesy according to the proportion of faith; Or ministry, let us wait on our ministering: or he that teacheth, on teaching; Or he that exhorteth, on exhortation: he that giveth, let him do it with simplicity; he that ruleth, with diligence; he that sheweth mercy, with cheerfulness. (Romans 12:4-8)

Paul wrote often about spiritual gifts. Three primary Scriptures teach us about these gifts of the spirit: Romans 12:4-8; 1 Corinthians 12:4-11; and Ephesians 4:7-13. The Lord placed these gifts within the body of Christ to enable believers to perform tasks that would help the church and edify (build up) the believer, which glorifies God. We are all born with certain innate qualities that often lie dormant and hidden within us, and we seek desperately to find our purpose in life. Those who have failed in this quest or in receiving spiritual gifts should pray, for God will surely answer. Many schools and churches offer tests to determine our gifts and purpose.

Every person has gifts, talents, and strengths, and the Bible helps us to discover these, as well as the calling God gives us to use these qualities to His glory. While you expand your mind and prepare for the future, you will come to understand more about God's purpose for your life. Knowing what God wants you to do brings satisfaction and fulfillment.

Devotional focus:

I believe it would be beneficial to imagine a common situation that many of us have witnessed. You may see yourself somewhere in this scenario. Picture a college cafeteria on the first day of classes. A nervous freshman walks along with a food tray. As she reaches a table, her attention strays away for a moment and she places only part of the tray on the table. It suddenly crashes to the floor. The whole cafeteria stops for a moment, as people notice her embarrassment. Then, everyone resumes eating. This unlikely place may reveal a person's gifts. Notice the way people respond to her, and remember the manifestations of the Spirit listed in Romans 12.

The person with the mercy gift may show up first. This person offers comfort and empathizes with the freshman. The person with the serving gift (ministry) may say, "Let me help you clean that up." The person with a teaching gift may remind her to put the tray down carefully next time before looking around the room. The person with a prophetic gift may say, "I saw you putting it down and knew that that would happen." The person with an administration gift (ruling) would show up and take charge. The administrator would quickly give assignments to get everything back to normal. The person with a giving gift would offer to get another tray and, if necessary, pay for the food. The person with the gift of encouraging (exhorting) would tell the freshman that it could happen to anyone, not to worry. Where do you see yourself in that scenario?

We need to ask ourselves if we feel drawn to a certain group of people or a certain place. We should look at the activities we do that bring enjoyment, affirmation, and fulfillment, thinking about those at which we excel. We often discover our purpose and gifts in the most unlikely places.

Journal reflection:

____

____

____

____

____

____

Chapter Eight

Avoiding Dangerous Pitfalls

1. *Standing Strong*
2. *The Plastic Trap*
3. *Mr. Broadminded*
4. *Dating Dynamics*
5. *Keep Your Head If You Lose Your Heart*
6. *Out of Control*
7. *Campus Bonfire*

Voices and Choices

"I chose some of the wrong friends. This hurt me. I had to make new friends."

"I would say that a lot of times we do things because of peer pressure. We do those things because we want to fit in with a group. This causes us a lot of problems and leads to some big mistakes."

"It is easy to be distracted, but don't be distracted from the things that are important."

"I went to school to party. I had to buckle down."

"It seems like you have to party to be popular on my campus. Alcohol and drugs are everywhere. You have to resist those things and stand on what you believe."

Journal Focus

Let's face it. You'll have many opportunities to act in a way that will get you off track. List some of the ways that you can show spiritual discipline in avoiding harmful distractions.

Strength Through Prayer

"Dear Lord, please remind me that I do not have to participate in sinful activities to fit into a group. Lord, I need the right kind of friends, and I know that you will send them. Please help me to stand against the things that are wrong. Amen."

Standing Strong

Scriptural insight:

And after him was Shammah. . . . And the Philistines were gathered together into a troop, where was a piece of ground full of lentiles: and the people fled from the Philistines. But he stood in the midst of the ground, and defended it, and slew the Philistines: and the Lord wrought a great victory. (2 Samuel 23:11-12)

At my first answer no man stood with me, but all men forsook me. . . . Notwithstanding the Lord stood with me, and strengthened me. (2 Timothy 4:16-17)

Shammah, an Old Testament hero about whom we know little, appears suddenly in the Bible on a list of mighty men of valor. His claim to fame: he took a stand against an enemy called "the Philistines." This people seemed constantly to threaten Israel, sending both organized armies and small groups of marauding soldiers against it. Shammah had witnessed the devastation that years of warfare with this enemy had brought. He had seen them steal the crops, fruits, and herds of his homeland. When the Philistines approached his lentil field to take his crop, everyone but Shammah fled. He knew they outnumbered him, but he stood strong in the midst of his lentil field. Not only did he hold his ground, but he also defeated the enemy and preserved what he considered to be precious.

Paul, a well-known New Testament hero about whom we know a great deal, cites an incident in his life that, apparently, had troubled him. When others should have supported and encouraged him, they seem to have forsaken him. His story, however, ended on a happy note, for he tells us that the "Lord stood with me, and strengthened me." As he faced the enemy, he may have felt alone. He suddenly realized, however, that the Lord stood with him. He received strength through the unseen presence of the Lord.

As Christians, we have Jesus' assurance that He will always be with us. If you ever feel you're all alone, just remember His promise: "I will never leave thee, nor forsake thee" (Hebrews 13:5).

Devotional focus:

As we talked to students for this book, we found it amazing that so many of them made the same comments. Several students talked about having to stand all alone for what they believe. One senior put it this way, "I go to a secular rather than a Christian school, and it seems you have to party to be popular on my campus. A lot of clubs throw drinking parties. Alcohol and drugs are everywhere. Acceptance is based on drinking. Doing the right thing means you're on your own. It's easy to fall away from your Christian foundation. You have to resist those things and stand on what you believe."

All of us want friends, and we want to be popular. These needs have caused many to make terrible mistakes. Friendship and popularity often come at too high a price. Some lose their health, become addicted, become pregnant, contract a sexually transmitted disease, or even lose their life because they made bad choices. We must refuse to exchange our Christian faith for these temptations. Although we find some temptations hard to resist, we must stand strong for what we believe. We must remember that we always have the best friend we could ever find standing with us (Proverbs 18:24).

Journal reflection:

The Plastic Trap

Scriptural insight:

Now there cried a certain woman of the wives of the sons of the prophets unto Elisha, saying, Thy servant my husband is dead; and thou knowest that thy servant did fear the Lord: and the creditor is come to take unto him my two sons to be bondmen. (2 Kings 4:1)

The rich ruleth over the poor, and the borrower is servant to the lender. (Proverbs 22:7)

Owe no man any thing, but to love one another. (Romans 13:8)

God often used the prophet Elisha in extraordinary ways. On one occasion, a desperate mother approached him and began to plead for his help. Her husband had apparently borrowed some money but had passed away before repaying the loan. The creditor had the right to take her children away from her. The labor of her children as servants would serve as repayment of the loan.

In delivering her from a desperate situation, God performed one of the most amazing miracles of the Bible. Elisha told her to borrow vessels and begin filling them from a vessel of oil within her home. She started pouring the oil, and it flowed until she had filled all the vessels. She sold the oil and paid the creditor. God removed the debt and the desperation from her life.

We often read about money in the Bible. The Word of God informs us that those who loan us money have power over us. The debt we have incurred makes us a servant to others. So the Bible encourages us to be good stewards, using wisdom in the way we handle financial matters.

Devotional focus:

The department head had heard about a study regarding students failing to finish undergraduate school. She said, "More college students drop out because of credit card debt than any other reason." Stress and pressure, along with personal, family, and moral problems, certainly take their toll and cause many to withdraw early. Debt, however, ranks as the number one reason why most students quit.

Mismanaging funds also causes the most divorces. Some husbands and wives wreck their marriages, because they fail to discipline themselves in financial management. Often, new families charge items as they try to accumulate possessions. Remember, your parents amassed their belongings over many years. Credit cards can help you out of a jam, but they can also get you into a jam. For many of us, they become plastic traps that can strip us of our dreams and place our life and future into terrible bondage.

Does this describe your life? If so, you should be ready to make some drastic changes. Do you feel that you can practice discipline in the area of financial management? Are you able to say "no" to constant shopping and "no" to picking up items you feel you must have? Do you want to salvage your future dreams and finish school with a degree? Do you want to save yourself from the pain and pressure of being too short of cash to make future payments? Begin by paying off the credit card with the smallest balance. See if you can have any of the rates lowered on the other credit cards that you hold. Practice discipline and be determined to conquer the temptation to "just charge it." Pray about your debt, and expect God to give you a miracle.

Journal reflection:

____

____

____

____

____

____

____

Mr. Broadminded

Scriptural insight:

Beware lest any man spoil you through philosophy and vain deceit, after the tradition of men, after the rudiments of the world, and not after Christ. (Colossians 2:8)

Beware! You might expect to hear that word if you were to walk into a yard that had a large, ferocious dog or to see the word if you were to venture into a construction area. You might not, however, imagine that it would be in the pages of God's Word. Even so, the Bible uses "beware" 27 times.

Paul, in talking to the church at Colosse, expressly used that word to alert these believers to a real danger. Many different gods and beliefs about worship filled their world and directly contradicted the Bible. To embrace various gods, beliefs, and practices of worship contradictory to the Bible would be destructive. So Paul cautioned the early church to be on guard, sober, and alert—to beware.

The pages of God's Word often flash a warning light concerning false teachers and our beliefs. What we believe does affect our lives. Beware lest new thoughts and ideas move you away from God and His word.

Devotional focus:

As a college freshman, excited about all his new courses, he soon discussed his philosophy class with other students, sharing some questions from the class. "Can God make a rock He cannot move?" "What happens when the unstoppable force meets the immovable object?" Instead of his questions boggling my mind, impressing me, or perplexing me, I remembered the Bible's warning to avoid foolish questions (Titus 3:9 and 2 Timothy 2:23). Another student, working on his master's degree, had to take philosophy. He numbly stumbled up to me and talked about the class and then said, "I don't know what to believe anymore." Certainly, being exposed to various religions, ideas, and the critiquing of the Bible had damaged his faith.

Every student stretches and broadens his mind, but we need to broaden our minds without becoming broadminded. School teaches us to think. Our degree reflects the level of our academic studies. Often, we find our absolutes and values to be challenged and changed. What are your core values? Do you believe that God created the heavens and the earth? When evolutionists talk, I often think about the just-right size of the sun and how God placed it at precisely the right distance. Tidal waves or water stagnation would result were the size or position of the moon different. The trillions of stars and the order of creation also come to mind.

Do you believe that Jesus was God's only Son and that He died and rose again? Prophecy, history, and witnesses verify these facts. Do you believe the Bible to be God's Holy Word? The Bible has withstood every attack and continues to be the most published book in the world. Heaven and earth shall pass, but His words will not pass away (Matthew 24:35).

Fundamentalism may be mocked and unpopular, but fundamental beliefs make a healthy and vital Christian. Broaden your mind, of course, but keep the absolutes from God's Word. I absolutely believe in absolutes.

Journal reflection:

____

____

____

____

____

____

____

____

Dating Dynamics

Scriptural insight:

And the Lord God said, It is not good that the man should be alone; I will make him an help meet for him. (Genesis 2:18)

And the Lord God caused a deep sleep to fall upon Adam, and he slept: and he took one of his ribs, and closed up the flesh instead thereof; And the rib, which the Lord God had taken from man, made he a woman, and brought her unto the man. (Genesis 2:21-22)

The Bible teaches us that God ordains marriage. In a day when people seem to devalue and discard marriage, we must remember that God planned this holy practice. The familiar story of Adam and Eve reveals that God recognized a deep need within Adam not to be alone. So God made Eve. Countless ladies have speculated that God practiced on Adam and got it right when He created Eve. I've even heard them say that practice makes perfect.

Most singles today want to get married. In fact, many popular Web sites and dating services specialize in matching you with a compatible person. Multitudes use these avenues to search for a mate. God made us with social needs to be met through family and friends, and God made us with sexual needs to be met only in marriage. Single people often fail to realize that God knows about their deepest needs. Feelings of desperation and depression often make them feel that no one could love or want them. Long before your birth, however, God had a plan for your life. You must trust God and have confidence that He will work all things together for your good at the right time (Romans 8:28).

One graduate had turned 26 before he left for college, and he wondered about God's plan for his life. Not until his junior year did he meet his future bride. At seven years younger, she joked that he had to wait for her to grow up. Their union has brought them happiness and contentment. For many years, he wondered about God's plan, but he finally realized that God had a perfect plan for him after all.

Devotional focus:

Dating can be fun and exciting, or it can be painful and unpleasant. The choices you make determine the outcome. We want to share some simple lessons to help you formulate a dating strategy. We know that many books focus on being single, on dating, and on relationships. In fact, many college students have enough dating experience to write their own book, but other students have little knowledge about the custom. These lessons may reinforce some reports you've heard or share a few lessons that are new to you.

- While waiting for the right person, you must focus on becoming the best person you can be. Continue to grow, learn, and develop.
- Avoid rushing into a relationship because you feel desperate. The pain you receive from a bad relationship can be greater than the ache of remaining single.
- Refuse to retreat from others because of your shyness or your feeling that no one is interested in you. You have to get out there to meet someone.
- Never date someone you would refuse to marry. Why would you become emotionally involved or hurt them?
- Know when to run away if your relationship turns abusive or harmful. Withdraw from dangerous people. Run like the wind!
- Stay away from dangerous places that increase your chances of being harmed.
- Look deeper than the surface of another person. He or she may have many wonderful qualities that you will learn about only if you take time to talk.
- Pray about God's will regarding the people you date.
- Trust God's plan for your life. He always exercises perfect timing.
- You may have a low-cost but still wonderful date, thanks to creative ideas. Remember, many campus activities are free.

Journal reflection:

Keep Your Head If You Lose Your Heart

Scriptural insight:

Then said Boaz unto his servant that was set over the reapers, Whose damsel is this? (Ruth 2:5)

So Boaz took Ruth, and she was his wife. (Ruth 4:13)

The Bible contains some of the greatest romance stories of all times—for instance, the story of Boaz and Ruth. A successful landowner and farmer, Boaz had his mind on checking his fields, part of his daily routine, rather than on marriage. Ruth may well have still been grieving over the loss of her husband and needed to find food for herself and her mother-in-law. Then, Ruth and Boaz suddenly discovered each other, as Ruth worked in one of his fields. You can tell that she quickly caught his eye. As soon as he noticed her, he had to know her name.

I believe that God arranged this meeting. He sees our deepest needs and works in many invisible ways to meet them. At the time, we may fail to notice His hand at work in our lives. When we look back, however, we can recognize His providential help at strategic moments. We may accomplish some things by design, but often we seem to stumble into other successful accomplishments. God works to our good whether we discern His assistance, or He keeps it hidden. His designed plan for us will bring us joy and fulfillment. This classic story of romance has a happy ending. Boaz and Ruth married and later Ruth gave birth to a little boy who became part of the lineage of Jesus.

Devotional focus:

Love stories and romance certainly draw everyone's attention. The fairy-tale-type marriage of Prince Charles to Lady Diana caught the attention of the entire world. Millions watched as they exchanged marital vows. Everyone dreams of a fairy-tale-type romance. Deep in our hearts, we long for someone to meet all of our emotional, physical, and spiritual needs, for someone to share our dreams, listen to us, and love us.

We experience a wonderful feeling of exhilaration when a member of the opposite sex notices us. Anticipating a first date may be overwhelming, but later we find it fulfilling to discover shared similarities, interests, and values. Those falling in love often daydream and picture their lives together. Many students, however, exploit others, preying on those needs and feelings. Every school has students who use and abuse others for their own gratification. Often, a romantic relationship may prove harmful and destructive.

If you're losing your heart, please don't lose your head. Ask yourself some questions. Have you prayed about your relationship? Does the association build self-esteem and self-respect or does it tear you down? Can you control your emotions and meet the responsibilities of your classes? Do you have the willpower to tell him or her that you have work to do and will see them later? Is your romance enhancing your educational experience or destroying it? Do you have the resolve to break up a destructive relationship? Do you have the determination to keep your head as you balance school and romance?

Journal reflection:

____

____

____

____

____

____

____

____

Out of Control

Scriptural insight:

He that hath no rule over his own spirit is like a city that is broken down, and without walls. (Proverbs 25:28)

But I keep under my body, and bring it into subjection: lest that by any means, when I have preached to others, I myself should be a castaway. (1 Corinthians 9:27)

The Bible never tries to hide the fact that temptations allure men and women (James 1:13-15). Neither does it hide that engaging in sin can be pleasurable (Hebrews 11:25). In fact, I've heard many speakers say, "Don't tell me that I didn't have fun when I was out in sin!" The same speakers revealed that, while they found sin pleasurable, it impacted their lives in terrible ways. They told of the pain they suffered from addictions, alcoholism, crimes, broken families, and broken lives.

The Bible talks about the destructive power of sin. It continually shares the fatality of sin's consequences. Notice some of the words the Bible uses to describe those in its awful grip: subjects (Romans 6:12), servants (Romans 6:17), dominion (Romans 6:14), and death (Romans 6:23). Paul recognized that temptation and sin could even cause him to become a castaway. He tells us that he had to practice spiritual discipline in order to keep himself from falling. He brought his body under control and kept it under subjection.

If you ever found yourself a prisoner of war, kidnapped, or tied up, you would struggle to free yourself. The Bible informs us that God offers spiritual freedom, and you can avoid the pain and destructive consequences of sin. Like Paul, we must practice spiritual discipline to maintain our freedom.

Devotional focus:

The student, part of the work-study program, had a job working as a groundskeeper. One day, he placed a lot of rubbish in the back of the old army truck that belonged to the school. As he drove toward the trash dump, the truck's brakes suddenly failed. He put the brake pedal to the floor but the huge, heavy vehicle refused to slow down.

A feeling of helplessness swept over the student. He knew this could be a terrible disaster, if anyone got in his way. Thankfully, he met little traffic and pulled into an empty parking lot, slowed down, and stopped. He breathed a sigh of relief.

Being out of control creates an awful feeling. That incident seems to capture the spiritual climate that exists on many campuses today. Just exchange the story of the army truck for an out-of- control life. The debauchery that occurs on many campuses boggles the mind. The tragedy, violence, and loss of life sadden our hearts. If you find yourself out of control and in danger of crashing, pull over immediately. Put on the brakes and save yourself from becoming a spiritual or educational accident victim.

Journal reflection:

Campus Bonfire

Scriptural insight:

And many that believed came, and confessed, and shewed their deeds. Many of them also which used curious arts brought their books together, and burned them before all men: and they counted the price of them, and found it fifty thousand pieces of silver. (Acts 19:18-19)

Our family rarely has the opportunity to go camping. Whenever we do, we look for firewood as soon as we set up the campsite. After dark, we love to build a big, roaring fire. It helps to drive away the bugs and keep us warm, as the night air turns cooler. When I served as a youth pastor, our group built a big bonfire and roasted marshmallows and wieners. We sang and shared stories around the flames. What great memories!

Believers in Ephesus built a giant bonfire, too, but this one, rather than roasting marshmallows and wieners or warming people and driving away bugs, helped destroy the evil influence in the lives of some young converts. This flame marked a total break from an idol god and wicked influences. They burned their bridges behind them. Can you imagine their countenances as they gazed into the bonfire, its flames flickering upon their faces? We can picture some of the city's many prostitutes watching tearfully as their sinful trappings turned to ashes. As the books blazed and images of idols melted, I believe the people rejoiced.

The Bible does teach us to depart from iniquity (2 Timothy 2:19). It also teaches us that we should give no place to evil within our lives (Ephesians 4:27). It tells us that sin should not reign over us (Romans 6:12). All of us must rid ourselves of wicked pleasures if we want to be free spiritually. While an actual bonfire may be out of reach, you can still use a trash can.

Devotional focus:

If you burn trash in a city, you will probably need a permit. When a university decides to have a bonfire, it may need a fire chief's permission. Fire presents an extremely dangerous situation, so you must exercise great caution when lighting a bonfire. I wish students would ask for a permit for a bonfire. The kind I'm picturing would be safe, of course, and it would be for a specific purpose. Some pages of pornographic magazines would serve as kindling. Books that influence perverse sexual behavior, violence, and anti-God thoughts would serve as the wood. Music that leads to perversion and to disrespect for women could also fuel the flame. Some drug paraphernalia and alcohol cans or bottles would make the bonfire complete. As flames played upon the faces of those in the crowd, I believe I would see some tears and smiles. A voice in the crowd might say, "I'm so glad I am free!"

You may never have a bonfire to burn evil influences. You can, however, make the choice to rid yourself of anything that may ultimately destroy your life.

Journal reflection:

___

___

___

___

___

___

___

___

___

___

Chapter Nine

Strength to Face the Stress

1. *The Face in the Mirror*
2. *Isolation and Participation*
3. *At the Breaking Point*
4. *Facing Monumental Challenges*
5. *Your Hidden Strength*
6. *The Strength to Face Another Day*
7. *Lost on Campus*

Voices and Choices

"I had to push myself to get out of my room and make some new friends."

"The university offers a lot of mixer-type activities. At the very least, you will get lots of free food."

"Find a mentor. A mentor will give you advice and hold you accountable."

"When I came to school, I isolated myself. I had to push myself to try out for a vocal group. You've got to put yourself out there."

"You are stronger than you think. You can accomplish more than you realize."

Journal Focus

How do you feel at this point in the semester? By now, most students feel drained. Make some journal entries about how you can restore your strength.

Strength Through Prayer

"Dear Father, midterm examinations have left me feeling exhausted. I pray that You will strengthen me as I face the second half of this semester. Amen."

The Face in the Mirror

Scriptural insight:

And the angel of the Lord appeared unto him, and said unto him, The Lord is with thee, thou mighty man of valour. (Judges 6:12)

And he said unto him, Oh my Lord, wherewith shall I save Israel? Behold, my family is poor in Manasseh, and I am the least in my father's house. (Judges 6:15)

Were you to look in the Bible for a hero, you might completely pass over Gideon. He himself acknowledged his limited ability. When an angel found his hiding place, Gideon reacted with great timidity, and their conversation revealed poor self-esteem and his lack of confidence. He may have thought others could achieve greatness, but he discounted his ability to accomplish any significant act. He saw himself as a weakling and a wimp. Others may have felt the same way about him. Had you questioned his family about his leadership ability, they may have reflected the same sentiments that Gideon expressed—great doubt about what he could accomplish. Few would ever have thought he would become one of Israel's legendary heroes.

The words that God gave Samuel might also be said of Gideon: "For the Lord seeth not as man seeth; for man looketh on the outward appearance, but the Lord looketh on the heart" (1 Samuel 16:7). God saw Gideon's heart, and God saw a potential hero. The angel told Gideon what God thought about him, that He recognized him as a brave and valiant man, one with potential. Gideon needed to hear that word from the Lord, as God worked to build his self-esteem. Events soon revealed that God knew Gideon's true character from the start, as God used Gideon in an unprecedented way to bring a great deliverance from the enemy. I feel certain that Gideon never again looked at himself in the same way.

Devotional focus:

The chapel speaker held up a tape measure. To illustrate feelings of low self-esteem, he pulled out about three feet of the tape, saying that we often feel that we fail to measure up to others and that we limit ourselves with our lack of confidence.* Low self-esteem and a lack of confidence cause countless numbers to stand before their mirror and see themselves as wimps, weaklings, and failures. Many focus on their shortcomings rather than their strengths, never considering what gifts they possess. Many people rarely dream of great accomplishments. They remind me of Gideon: "I could never go to college!" "I could never make it on my own!" "I'm not as smart as these other students!" "I'm not as pretty as that girl!"

The Bible teaches us that God sees our great potential. He sees you surviving the transition of moving away from your family and friends and into a dorm. He sees you completing research papers and passing difficult tests. He sees you growing in confidence and ability. He sees you living a successful and joyous life. You may think it trite and elementary, but the next time you look in a mirror realize that God sees you as a hero.

* Taken from a thought by Pastor Jentezen Franklin.

Journal reflection:

____

____

____

____

____

____

____

____

____

Isolation and Participation

Scriptural insight:

Know ye not that they which run in a race run all, but one receiveth the prize? So run, that ye may obtain. And every man that striveth for the mastery is temperate in all things. . . . I therefore so run, not as uncertainly; so fight I, not as one that beateth the air. (1 Corinthians 9:24-26)

The Apostle Paul loved to use symbols to illustrate a point. He talked about running in a race. He talked about fighting and shadow boxing. He talked about a soldier wearing armor and the Christian being clothed in spiritual armor. He talked about wrestling. These military and sport images have a common theme. They relate to the Christian enduring in spiritual warfare with the enemy. These images not only show us the importance of enduring and persevering, but they also demonstrate that being victorious and successful takes great effort.

Athletes and warriors rarely achieve success by accident, and it takes more than entering a contest to win an award. The runner, wrestler, and soldier all must apply themselves. They must push themselves to the edge of their endurance to become competent in their endeavor and to triumph.

Devotional focus:

The university junior discussed with me the toughest situation she had faced. She openly told me about being shy and about the difficulty she had in making new friends. As she began her educational experience, she spent most of her time in her room, seldom speaking to others. She shed many tears as she thought about being at home.

She had important advice to others who have chosen to stay isolated in a dorm room. She knew that this book would offer help to students just like her. She wanted me to share how she survived and how she made an adjustment that led to finding happiness and tranquility. Her simple yet profound advice for students: "Push yourself!" She said, "I had to push myself to get out of my room and make friends." She discussed the importance of moving out of your comfort zone. Other students echoed the same feelings. One student said, "The university offers a lot of mixer-type activities. At the very least, you will get lots of free food!" She had to push herself to make friends, get involved, and leave her isolated comfort zone.

You may find this decision a little frightening, as you encounter groups that may be a poor fit for you. You will probably meet people who give you a cold shoulder. But what do you have to lose? The four walls of a dorm room can never listen to you, share interesting thoughts and important feelings, or empathize with you. So, push yourself from isolation and move toward participation. Discover the joy of knowing others who, just like you, want to make a new friend.

Journal reflection:

At the Breaking Point

Scriptural insight:

A bruised reed shall he not break. (Matthew 12:20)

There hath no temptation taken you but such as is common to man: but God is faithful, who will not suffer you to be tempted above that ye are able; but will with the temptation also make a way to escape, that ye may be able to bear it. (1 Corinthians 10:13)

Who would have thought that Jesus would have used so many everyday objects to teach spiritual lessons? For instance, He used a child to instruct us on humility (Matthew 18:2-6). He used seed to tutor us on receiving the gospel (Matthew 13:3-9). He used sheep to educate us on our value (Luke 15:4-7). He used a mountain to lecture about faith (Matthew 21:21). He used a reed to tell us about God's mercy and grace. Similar to bamboo plants, reeds grew abundantly along the Jordan River, so the people used them in various ways. Jesus used a reed to illustrate how God responds to those who have been wounded. Rather than finishing off the wounded, He lifts and heals them (Luke 10:33-35; Isaiah 42:3). Paul told us that the Lord can make a way of escape even before a person receives deadly wounds. In the same way, the Lord can help us flee the destructive power of temptation and help us withstand it without breaking.

Devotional focus:

The breaking point! This is an emotional location that none of us wants to reach and a dangerous place that has serious consequences. A breaking point may occur when we overfill our schedules, when demands on us exceed our time limit, and when we get too little rest. Symptoms that we have reached this dangerous state may include irrational behavior, a flood of tears, mistreating those we love, and a feeling of panic. You may have experienced some of these characteristics or witnessed them in others. At a breaking point, a sense of desperation grips you, and you feel as though you may fall apart, that you may not survive. When you find yourself at the breaking point, please remember these facts:

- The sun will come up tomorrow. This is not the end of the world.
- Others have survived and so will you.
- You can handle much more than you realize.
- You have already survived many difficult challenges.
- In a few days, this semester or quarter will be over.
- Reading the Bible and praying will refresh you.
- God will help you to bear the pressure without breaking.

Why not look right now at what David said about his survival and his escape in Psalm 124?

Journal reflection:

Facing Monumental Challenges

Scriptural insight:

And there went out a champion out of the camp of the Philistines, named Goliath. (1 Samuel 17:4)

Then said David to the Philistine, Thou comest to me with a sword, and with a spear, and with a shield: but I come to thee in the name of the Lord of hosts, the God of the armies of Israel, whom thou hast defied. (1 Samuel 17:45)

So David prevailed over the Philistine with a sling and with a stone, and smote the Philistine, and slew him. (1 Samuel 17:50)

People love to cheer for their favorite hero. Movies offer a variety of champions known for their courage. Hollywood special effects give us many larger-than-life characters who survive all odds and emerge safe and sound. The drama of a great white shark caught the public's attention some years ago, as three men fought against this massive creature in an epic battle for survival. Some people still have trouble going into the ocean because of the movie *Jaws*.

The media often overlooks real stories of heroism, but a few accounts do make the news, perhaps even the headlines. Hearing that someone survived overwhelming odds inspires us. The Bible tells us an inspiring story about a teenager who made the news in Israel and had everyone talking about it (1 Samuel 18:6-7). The scene represents drama at its best. Two armies face each other. A great warrior named "Goliath" stands and mocks God and threatens the army of Israel. No one could possibly have anticipated what would happen next. A teenager who had spent his life as a shepherd suddenly asks to confront the giant. The mighty men of Israel cower in fear, but this shepherd boy demonstrates great daring. Thousands watch as the drama unfolds with the youth facing the seasoned warrior. They sneer at each other and share some threats. Soon, the massive giant hits the ground, and David stands on his dead body. Giants failed to terrorize David. He faced Goliath with confidence that God would help him. David became one of the greatest true-life heroes of all time.

Devotional focus:

Bravery may be found on a battlefield, as well as on many college campuses. Students have left the security of home for the anxieties of college. Many have left parents with health issues, and some have left a single parent. Scores face financial challenges. Most would find it far easier to stay home. A campus compares well to a battlefield in terms of survival.

God rewarded the boldness of David, and He has respect for no particular person (Acts 10:34). He will honor those who bravely pursue His purposes for their lives. He will help those who courageously trust Him, strengthening them to stand against the menacing giants of today (Ephesians 6:11). As you face the monumental challenges of your life, remember that God still topples giants. He still gives great victories to underdogs.

Journal reflection:

Your Hidden Strength

Scriptural insight:

And when the sun was up, they were scorched; and because they had no root, they withered away. (Matthew 13:6)

As ye have therefore received Christ Jesus the Lord, so walk ye in him: Rooted and built up in him, and stablished in the faith, as ye have been taught, abounding therein with thanksgiving. (Colossians 2:6-7)

An amazing event has just happened. It occurred across our country in many locations. All of us witnessed it, but few of us thought about it. I'm talking about the return of spring and the great change in nature. Hundreds of trees stand behind our home. I've watched their barren branches suddenly explode into beautiful green foliage. This remarkable change in nature transpires only because of actions hidden from the natural eye. Above ground, we see barren branches put on new foliage, but we fail to see proceedings underground. Any class in botany teaches astounding information about root systems. They stabilize trees and collect massive amounts of water necessary for a tree's survival. You can see a wonderful plant display with visible roots at The Land Pavilion in Disney World. A boat ride takes you through various displays of plants hanging in the air with their root systems on display. Every time I have looked at these plants with vegetables hanging from them, I have been filled with awe. They seem to defy nature. Don't you need dirt to grow stuff?

The Bible uses roots as a way to illustrate life and stability. Jesus told us that plants with shallow roots quickly wither when the sun shines. Paul explained that, like a plant, we have a root system and ours connects to the Lord. A further study of this Bible analogy reveals that the Lord, though unseen, stabilizes, strengthens, and sustains us (John 15:1-5). True success in life only occurs when you have the right foundation (Matthew 7:24-27). Strength to withstand the crushing demands of life occurs when you have the right root system. Were I to ask you about your roots, I would be talking, not about your heritage, but about the source of your strength. Can you tell me about your roots?

Devotional focus:

Most of us know little about grass and have little interest in learning about it. We expect lawns to be beautiful automatically. Few of us aerate or over-seed in the fall. We rarely add lime or fertilizer to nourish the soil for our grass. We seldom irrigate during a drought. It's a wonder we have grass on our lawns at all. My neighbor knows a lot about lawns. He surprised me when he said, "Grass roots grow best in winter." After aeration, over-seeding, irrigating, adding lime, and fertilizing, these roots experience real growth during the freezing days of winter. As difficult as it may be to believe, neither heavy snow nor frozen ground prevents roots from flourishing. Grass roots experience their growing peak in the harsh winter months (close to the length of a semester).

I believe this winter analogy applies to life and especially to students (Ecclesiastes 3:1-8). In retrospect, school does seem somewhat like wintertime. Freezing temperatures and snows could represent testing; harsh winds, attending class. At times, students may feel the harmful effects of winter. However, they eventually realize that hard conditions have actually made them stronger. Wintry weather may seem difficult, but its value lies in your growth, development, and success.

Winter has one predictable aspect: it will end at the right time. Sometimes we despair that spring will ever arrive. Then, before we know it, all of nature bursts into life again. Your educational experience will be the same way. One day, your classes will end, and you will enter the springtime and summer of achieving your goals and dreams.

Journal reflection:

____

____

The Strength to Face Another Day

Scriptural insight:

And Moses said unto God, Who am I, that I should go unto Pharaoh, and that I should bring forth the children of Israel out of Egypt? (Exodus 3:11)

Then said the Lord unto Moses, Behold, I will rain bread from heaven for you; and the people shall go out and gather a certain rate every day. (Exodus 16:4)

Give us this day our daily bread. (Matthew 6:11)

He giveth power to the faint; and to them that have no might he increaseth strength. (Isaiah 40:29)

As Moses went about his daily routine of watching the sheep, he saw an extraordinary sight. He wanted a closer look and walked toward the flaming bush in the distance. The flame must have been captivating; the sound, startling. The voice suddenly emanating from within the bush told him to remove his shoes for he was standing in the presence of God on Holy Ground. God spoke and commissioned Moses to return to Egypt to deliver the children of Israel from bondage. Moses immediately started to doubt his ability to accomplish this assigned task and began to make excuses. God gave him visible and miraculous signs that let him know that He would be with him. Moses went, though reluctantly, and God supplied the necessary strength.

One of Moses' biggest tests in the wilderness related to a source of food for the people. Then, God rained down bread like snowflakes. This miracle provided nourishment and energy to face the new challenges of life. The manna fell from Sunday through Friday. (They rested on the Sabbath.) Like bread from heaven, the Lord gives His children new vigor each day, so they can meet their tests.

Devotional focus:

When our money runs low and bills pile up, we know that we must have help. We feel so happy and appreciative when we receive financial help and can pay our creditors. When our strength diminishes and pressure mounts, we seldom realize that God stands ready to help. We often face the demands of life without asking Him for His help, strength, and assistance. Many Scriptures remind us that God wants to help us. Psalm 121:1-2, for instance, says, "I will lift up mine eyes unto the hills, from whence cometh my help. My help cometh from the Lord, which made heaven and earth." Prayer has brought needed help to the weak, to those in crises, and to those who need a miracle. The mighty weapon of prayer brings the resource of strength. Have you recognized the source of your strength to overcome doubts and fears and to meet the stressful demands of life? Have you prayed about the tests you face?

Journal reflection:

____

____

____

____

____

____

____

____

____

____

____

____

Lost on Campus

Scriptural insight:

Either what woman having ten pieces of silver, if she lose one piece, doth not light a candle, and sweep the house, and seek diligently till she find it? And when she hath found it, she calleth her friends and her neighbours together, saying, Rejoice with me; for I have found the piece which I had lost. (Luke 15:8-9)

Jesus taught three parables in Luke 15 about lost possessions. He talked about a lost sheep, a lost coin, and a lost son. His second parable focused on the lost coin. A woman had ten coins and suddenly found that she had lost one somewhere within her home. She valued the coin, so she lit a candle and began to search for it. She picked up her broom and began to sweep the floor. She found the coin and became so excited that she called her friends and asked them to celebrate with her. This parable teaches us that one coin has merit. The other parables in this chapter teach us that one sheep and one son also have significance. We learn that the Lord puts great effort into finding the spiritually lost, and that heaven rejoices when He does (Luke 15:22-23).

Devotional focus:

The word "lost" has numerous meanings. We may lose a possession or a direction, and we may be lost spiritually. I recently went for the first time to a large university. I needed an educational psychology text for one of the school's online classes. I failed to anticipate how difficult it would be to find the bookstore. The university has several campuses and about 55,000 students. I had a difficult time parking and an even more difficult time finding the bookstore. Before my visit was over, I got lost and had to ask directions.

A lot of students get lost on campus. I'm not talking about being a new student and having problems finding a classroom. I'm talking about students losing their direction academically and spiritually. We must face the facts. Lots of students begin college with great excitement and motivation. Then, the many opportunities to experiment with drugs, alcohol, and sex present themselves. Giving in to these temptations often has disastrous effects. Some addictions and habits become lifelong patterns.

A student spoke of visiting one school. He enjoyed all the activities they presented. He liked the academic opportunities available. He said, "I decided to spend some time on campus that night. It was a totally different place after dark. There was a lot of partying." He decided against that college because of some of the behavior he witnessed. He was letting me know that participating in such conduct would have changed the course of his life.

Academically, you must continue to apply yourself, and you must discipline yourself to stand against actions that could spoil your future. Spiritually, you must resist the "party spirit" that exists on many campuses and be "strong in the Lord" (Ephesians 6:10). Don't get lost on campus!

Journal reflection:

____

____

____

____

____

____

____

____

____

____

Chapter Ten

The Ability to Persevere

1. *The Temptation to Quit*
2. *Deferred Gratification*
3. *Marching Band Excellence*
4. *Unfinished Business*
5. *A Student Credo*
6. *Resilience Personified*
7. *The Potter's Process*

Voices and Choices

"I wanted to quit every semester."

"I'm going to survive by taking one thing at a time."

"Attitude is everything. You will not make it if you have a bad attitude."

"I've had to work my rear end off. It takes hard work to accomplish anything."

"Never give up."

"I've noticed that if I get down, it doesn't last for very long."

"Find a place that is conducive for study. Get a partner to study with. It helps me to make some note cards to remember things."

Journal Focus

Write some thoughts in your journal this week about the importance of enduring and being resilient. What are your thoughts about a student's need to exhibit resolve and tenacity?

Strength Through Prayer

"Heavenly Father, I know that anyone can quit. Quitting is easy and doesn't take any effort at all. Please teach me the importance of hanging in there when the going gets tough. Remind me that these lessons will be important later as I face some of the challenges of life. Amen."

The Temptation to Quit

Scriptural insight:

For Demas hath forsaken me, having loved this present world. (2Timothy 4:10)

Evangelists in the early church suffered a much harsher existence than they do today. Nowadays, those who evangelize in America rarely experience verbal attacks, and fewer still suffer physical assaults. At the time of the early church, however, evangelizing meant that a whole city might come out and protest against you (Acts 19:29), that you might be imprisoned (Acts 5:18), that you might lose your life (Acts 12:2).

A disciple named "Demas" had been a vital part of Paul's evangelistic team (Colossians 4:14). After some time had elapsed, he apparently became weary of ministry. It seems that worldly attractions enticed him, and he soon decided to quit. I doubt that he gave Paul a letter of resignation. Had he written one, it might have said, "Dear Paul, I have really enjoyed your company, but you know well our struggles and the hardships we have faced. The cost has been great; the rewards have been few. I quit! I will be pursuing some other avenues with my life. Your friend, Demas." Paul says little about this man who chose to give up. Wouldn't you love to have seen how he turned out? Wouldn't you love to know what consequences this terrible decision had? If he lived to be an old man, I believe he looked back at the moment that he quit as the biggest mistake of his life.

Devotional focus:

To be successful in any field or endeavor, you will have to hang in there. A farmer faces heat, rain, cold, and insects in his undertaking. An educator must pass many tests and keep teaching credentials current. Mechanics go through refresher courses to learn the latest technology. Doctors attend seminars and classes to learn about new methods and medicines. Ministers preach thousands of sermons that they must prayerfully develop. Countless illustrations show us that most careers require continuing efforts to be successful.

A man like Demas teaches us a valuable lesson. Despite having other options, he chose to quit. He could have asked Paul for help. He could have talked to someone about being tempted to give up. We may learn another vital lesson about quitting: **It often becomes a pattern that a person resorts to all of his life!** When events fail to suit him or the way becomes difficult, you can look for his resignation. When quitting becomes a pattern for a person's life, his education will suffer, his career will suffer, and his marriage will probably suffer.

The graduate spoke honestly when he said, "I wanted to quit every semester." He kept going, however, and learned that hard places made him stronger. He learned that difficult times eventually gave him greater ability. He learned that struggling through the challenges of life produced many valuable qualities that lead to a happy and successful life. He wanted to quit every semester, but he never did. Now, he feels joy and a sense of accomplishment because he persevered.

Journal reflection:

____

____

____

____

____

____

____

____

Deferred Gratification

Scriptural insight:

And the men of David said unto him, Behold the day of which the Lord said unto thee, Behold, I will deliver thine enemy into thine hand, that thou mayest do to him as it shall seem good unto thee. (1 Samuel 24:4)

Opportunities for great success and fame rarely come along. Nor do the opportunities to get even, dispose of one's enemies, or retaliate and be vindicated often present themselves. With one stroke of a knife, David had occasion to accomplish all these acts. Certainly, he would have been justified in the eyes of the people. After all, King Saul had treated him poorly, and was even trying to kill him. It would have been self-defense. Within his heart, however, David knew that God had anointed the king and had used him in a great way for Israel. He knew that he would be wrong to take King Saul's life. I'm sure David's decision to show mercy to his enemy met with contempt, as many people second-guessed him and wondered why he failed to act.

If you continue to read the narrative, you will discover that God promoted David in His own time. In his pursuit of God's perfect will, David chose to remain a fugitive—obscure, lonely, cold, and tearful. The pages of God's Word reveal that God eventually promoted David to the throne. I'm sure that David reflected upon His opportunities to kill Saul on many occasions and was glad that he had patiently waited for God to vindicate and promote him.

Devotional focus:

Her presence in a room always inspires me. I met her in her sophomore year of college. She wanted to be a medical doctor. She often talked about the difficulty of her classes and about the many hurdles that stood between her and her goal. She would, occasionally, make an eight-hour drive home from college. Gradually, she fulfilled all her responsibilities and graduated. Then, she enrolled in a medical school and faced new hurdles. Once she successfully met all those requirements, she faced another hurdle as she moved to yet another school to finish her education.

Somewhere along the way she fell in love, but she chose to put love and marriage on hold until she had accomplished her goals. Then, she had a beautiful wedding with a handsome and wonderful man, and now they have a son. Today, she works as a successful medical doctor and offers some sound advice to every student struggling to continue his or her education. "You must be determined if you are to accomplish your goals." She would also say that gratification and success certainly come to those determined to finish.

You will often have opportunities to jump ship and to seek immediate gratification, to forget your dreams and choose the path of least resistance. Many students, however, choose the path of deferred gratification. This path will take you through the weeks, months, and years you require to earn a degree. Following this path to its end will reward you with great fulfillment and future success.

Journal reflection:

Marching Band Excellence

Scriptural insight:

Furthermore then we beseech you, brethren, and exhort you by the Lord Jesus, that as ye have received of us how ye ought to walk and to please God, so ye would abound more and more. (1 Thessalonians 4:1)

Paul's letters often sought to discipline and correct early followers of Christ. Surprisingly, he dealt with a host of problems that existed in each of the churches. His letters do, however, contain loving words of appreciation and some encouraging words about his prayers for them. He attempted to solve problems and set the church in order. He even called by name some of those creating problems. His letters also contain often bold and confrontational warnings and rebukes.

Sometimes, leaders have no choice but to discipline and rebuke (Ephesians 4:15). Recipients have the opportunity to listen and to correct problems. They have the opportunity to receive instruction and move ahead without being offended. Constructive criticism may be painful, but it helps those who heed it.

Devotional focus:

Older students stood nose-to-nose with our son and yelled at him, and I did not like it. The scene looked like an Army boot camp with drill sergeants in control, as my wife and I stood along a fence and watched freshmen learning to march in the high school band. I could hardly believe my eyes. Other parents, too, showed their uneasiness. I first wanted to tell them that my son had not joined the marching band to be abused. Then, I realized that our son at 15 years of age would have to learn to fight his own battles. We refrained from interfering, but we fumed and fussed as we left school that day, noting that our son was giving them at least 40 hours of his time that week. I wondered why the school allowed such behavior.

Later in the week, I told my son how I felt and asked him if he wanted to stay with it. He informed me that this band had received many awards for being a marching band of excellence. It had for many years won some of Virginia's most outstanding awards. It had the reputation for being the best. He told me that the band members needed hard work, discipline, and correction to continue to be winners. He said, "Dad, if we can't hold up to the practice, how will we survive everything we'll have to face this year?" He had a point. They had to endure long practices and change many of their routines. They had to stand in the cold, rain, and snow at football games. They traveled near and far to perform and compete. In the years that followed, I watched him yell at the freshmen, helping them to learn to march with pride. The band continued to win the most prestigious awards in every competition that they entered.

Many times, as I watched them perform, I made spiritual comparisons. I thought about our need as Christians to challenge each other to do our best. I thought about the importance of enduring even when someone corrects us or makes us sad. I realized all Christians need to march in step and to please our heavenly director. Indeed, all of us should want excellence as we march through life.

Journal reflection:

____

____

____

____

____

____

____

____

____

Unfinished Business

Scriptural insight:

Being confident of this very thing, that he which hath begun a good work in you will perform it until the day of Jesus Christ. (Philippians 1:6)

But none of these things move me, neither count I my life dear unto myself, so that I might finish my course with joy, and the ministry, which I have received of the Lord Jesus, to testify the gospel of the grace of God. (Acts 20:24)

The words "determination," "perseverance," and "endurance" describe a person committed to a task. They also illustrate the tenacity of a committed Apostle named "Paul." The many candid snapshots that Paul gives us show the intensity of his great struggles. "I have fought with beasts at Ephesus" (1 Corinthians 15:32). "I have fought a good fight, I have finished my course." (2 Timothy 4:7). Another scene reveals that all hope for survival seemed to be gone (Acts 27:20). In yet another scene recorded in Corinthians, Paul says, "For we would not, brethren, have you ignorant of our trouble which came to us in Asia, that we were pressed out of measure, above strength, insomuch that we despaired even of life" (2 Corinthians 1:8). He seems to sum it all up by saying, "but none of these things move me." In spite of the struggles, he remained determined to finish his Christian race.

In comparing Paul's life-threatening situations to a student's journey toward graduation, we should consider that a student must also be determined to persevere and endure many hard times along the journey to graduation. Paul includes you and me as he thinks about finishing well. He lets us know that God began a work in us and that God will complete His work.

Devotional focus:

While starting a project or task may be easy, finishing it can prove difficult. That may be what the people who started painting the barn must have discovered. I've never stopped to ask them any questions about their project, as it's really none of my business. I do know that the sight of it greatly irritates me. Just driving past it upsets me. They painted the bottom half of the barn white and then stopped. The top has remained unpainted for 20 years or more. I've thought about taking some people with me and volunteering to finish the project or collecting money so they could pay to have it finished. Maybe I'll stop one day and ask about it. On second thought, I believe I'll just take another road next time I travel that way.

Scores of students begin their education, but never complete it. Startling statistics reveal that a little over half never finish. Sometimes, students have sound reasons for dropping out, perhaps sickness or health concerns. Many students quit, however, because they find the challenge too difficult or they never truly apply themselves. Unless you have a valid reason for quitting, please finish your education. Decline to allow the option of quitting to become a choice that defines your life. Quitting can become a way of life not only educationally, but also with a career or with a marriage. Refuse to allow your life to be like a half-painted barn.

Journal reflection:

____

____

____

____

____

____

____

____

A Student Credo

Scriptural insight:

Who shall separate us from the love of Christ? Shall tribulation, or distress, or persecution, or famine, or nakedness, or peril, or sword. . . . Nay, in all these things we are more than conquerors through him that loved us. For I am persuaded, that neither death, nor life, nor angels, nor principalities, nor powers, nor things present, nor things to come, Nor height, nor depth, nor any other creature, shall be able to separate us from the love of God, which is in Christ Jesus our Lord. (Romans 8:35-39)

Shortly after Paul's conversion to Christianity, God told him that he would undergo many terrible things (Acts 9:16). That revelation quickly became a reality. He reflects upon the sufferings he endured in one of his letters to the Corinthian church (2 Corinthians 11:23-27).

In pursuing the will of God, many of the Lord's disciples travel a pleasant path, while others travel a painful path. Yet, Paul reveals how resolute and confident he remains in the midst of his suffering. He boldly lists some of the adversaries and hardships that he has encountered. He broadens his thoughts as he includes us in his writings. Without hesitation, he asserts that none of those things would separate **us** from Christ. With great confidence, he affirms that **we** are more than conquerors through Him who loves **us**. These powerful words should strengthen our resolve as we face challenges. These insights should fill us with confidence and assurance as we withstand the tests and trials that come our way.

Devotional focus:

Often students begin their collegiate journey without declaring a major. After all, most degrees require some of the same basic courses. The decision of a major comes quickly for some, and it becomes a nightmare for others. Most students think only in the short term, rather than the long haul. You rarely find students who see the broad picture and who consider future classes or requirements. Just ask a university advisor about this problem. They will tell you they often hear students say, "I didn't know I had to do that, or I didn't know I had to take that course." Somebody obviously neglected to read the handbook that the institution provided. Some students struggle to have the tenacity to face the obstacles of the long haul. Tests, papers, projects, and requirements quickly overwhelm them. A few students quit before even getting a good start.

Paul gave us a good credo (belief/formula) for enduring as a Christian. He showed resolve through his sufferings. He let us know that we can conquer whatever comes our way, and that nothing can separate us from God's love. I think students need a credo for their journey. No tests, papers, projects, expectations, misunderstandings, temptations, doubts, or conflicts will separate you from finishing the collegiate journey before you.

Journal reflection:

Resilience Personified

Scriptural insight:

For a just man falleth seven times, and riseth up again. (Proverbs 24:16)

He restoreth my soul. (Psalm 23:3)

Most everyone takes a physical tumble now and then. Perhaps ice, snow, or a slippery spot causes us to go down, or a small stone, sand, or a turned up rug trips us. In severe cases, an orthopedic surgeon repairs the break and within weeks we resume walking. Emotional plunges occur when others hurt us. Often, they say or do something that disappoints us. We may feel wounded and wonder what happened. Counselors and friends help to pick us up. Most of us can function again, the event having made us stronger. Spiritual falls transpire when a traumatic spiritual event knocks us down. We may realize that we have failed God, others, and ourselves. These falls humiliate and embarrass us. The Bible tells us that the Lord wants to help those who have fallen spiritually to get back on their feet (1 John 2:1).

"Resilience" means bouncing back after hitting bottom, no matter what may have precipitated the fall. Solomon reminded us that a good man might be knocked down on numerous occasions but gets back on his feet. People stay down because they choose to give up. The many stories of the severely injured and handicapped have proven to us that resilient people can rise again.

Devotional focus:

In my opinion, Walter Payton personifies resilience. He had a 15-year football career with a total of 18,355 yards. He scored 164 touchdowns. He currently holds the record for the most yards and the most touchdowns in the NFL. His actual record of career rushes and yards per carry aside, let's say that someone tackled him every nine yards, to illustrate a point. That means he would hit the ground 2,039 times in his career. Though repeatedly thrown down, gouged, pushed, stepped on, bruised, and cut, he would continue to get back up.[1]

You may have failed a test, perhaps received a bad grade on a project paper. Maybe the clock failed to alarm, and you missed a vital class. A friend may have betrayed you. Someone may have gossiped about you. A girlfriend or boyfriend may have rejected you. Your family may be distancing themselves from you. You may have a big pimple on your nose. Many events can knock us down emotionally and spiritually. What do we do after our fall? We could choose to give up and quit. We could choose to feel sorry for ourselves. We could have a pity party. We could tell everyone how we have been wronged. Or we can choose to survive the event and rise up again.

The shepherd often used his staff to get cast sheep (those that were down) back on their feet. Often, these animals would have wobbly legs for a few minutes. They may have even collapsed again, but the shepherd would keep working with them. Such an occurrence inspired David to say, "He restoreth my soul" (Psalm 23:3).

We have all suffered traumatic falls of some sort. Let's allow the Good Shepherd to lovingly nurture resilience in our lives.

1. Walter Payton, *Wikipedia, The Free Encyclopedia, http: en.wikipedia.org/wiki/Walter Payton.html.*

Journal reflection:

____

____

____

____

____

____

____

The Potter's Process

Scriptural insight:

The word which came to Jeremiah from the Lord, saying, Arise, and go down to the potter's house, and there I will cause thee to hear my words. (Jeremiah 18:1-2)

Beloved, think it not strange concerning the fiery trial which is to try you, as though some strange thing happened unto you: But rejoice, inasmuch as ye are partakers of Christ's sufferings; that, when his glory shall be revealed, ye may be glad also with exceeding joy. (1 Peter 4:12-13)

We frequently use symbols to describe different times and events that occur in our lives. People having difficulty or pain might be said to be "in a valley." Those feeling exhilarated because they have accomplished some great feat might be said to be "on top of the world." The Bible, too, uses symbols. For instance, fire often signifies going through a difficult ordeal. Peter uses this symbol to describe persecution within the early church. Other writers use this same symbol to help us picture a trial we may be enduring. Going through the fire also represents the process of being refined or developed. Shadrach, Meshach, and Abednego had firsthand experience about going through the fire. They discovered protection in the fire, comfort in the fire, companionship in the fire, and deliverance from the fire (Daniel 3). Isaiah shared a promise from God for those who encounter fire. God has promised that He will see His children through the fire and the floods that come our way (Isaiah 43:2).

If fires of difficulty come your way, remember that these events occur for a reason. The process develops and refines you.

Devotional focus:

I've visited pottery stores and watched a potter mold and shape the clay. I've talked with shop owners and listened as they explained the process of "throwing pots." In addition, I've read many articles about pottery. This practice makes a good illustration for your educational process. At the beginning, the ugly lump of clay seems to have little potential. The potter looks at his material and imagines what it will become. He places it in the center of his wheel and begins spinning. Everything seems to be out of control for the clay, as the potter pokes, pushes, and pressures it into a shape. As the spinning continues, the potter looks for imperfections. He may even have to start over. Once he forms the clay, he paints it and then places it into the searing heat of the kiln. The process turns the clay into a lovely vessel. I asked a potter what would happen if he left the vessel in the kiln too long. He said the high heat would destroy it. The potter knows when to remove his work of art from the oven.

Every student sometimes feels his life spinning out of control. Students identify with feeling poked, pushed, and pressured. They experience great discomfort when they feel the heat turned up. It often seems to fill students with despair. The next time you feel the pain of the process, try to remember that the potter sees what you will become. His process of shaping you will make you into a vessel of honor (2 Timothy 2:21).

Journal reflection:

____

____

____

____

____

____

____

____

____

Chapter Eleven

The Practice of Spiritual Discipline

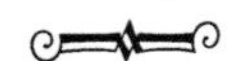

1. *The Discovery of a Lifetime*
2. *An Invitation From the King*
3. *The Ultimate Textbook*
4. *Student Aid*
5. *My Guidance Counselor*
6. *Your Father Knows*
7. *How Big Is Your God?*

Voices and Choices

"My values are different from lots of students. This has made it harder to make friends."

"What is really missing from a lot of lives is intrinsic values."

"I was very active in my youth group. My college is not religious. This made it hard to find a group to fit with."

"You will find what you are looking for at a school."

"I was sheltered growing up. I have a Christian background. I'm attending a non-Christian university, and it is hard to find Christian friends."

"I found a good church to get involved with. This helped me in many ways."

Journal Focus

Make a list of what's most important in your life. Does your list include any spiritual values? Write down some ways that you can grow in your walk with the Lord.

Strength Through Prayer

"Lord, my life is changing in so many ways. Don't let any of these changes distract me from serving You. Don't let me forsake the beliefs that I know are right. I pray that You would help me to establish some spiritual priorities. Please keep me from being drawn away from my relationship with You. Amen."

The Discovery of a Lifetime

Scriptural insight:

Philip findeth Nathanael, and saith unto him, We have found him, of whom Moses in the law, and the prophets, did write, Jesus of Nazareth, the son of Joseph. (John 1:45)

Some people experience wealth and fame through a discovery. One company even advertises its services for those who bring their new ideas and findings to the firm for development, manufacturing, and marketing. I read about a man who found a wonderful object. For years, he had walked back and forth over a bridge. One day, he stopped along the water's edge and noticed a big chunk of gold. You need not be an entrepreneur or explorer to make discoveries in life. You will encounter them all along the way.

Several students talked to us about some surprising revelations. When one student went to arrange payments for his school loans, he learned that someone had paid all of them for him. Another student found that someone had awarded him a scholarship without his knowledge. Last night, I heard that someone had gotten engaged and would be planning a wedding.

Spiritual discoveries often surprise us most. Realizing that God has revealed mysteries to us may overwhelm us (Matthew 13:11). Philip learned one day that the Messiah had arrived. He went and told his friend Nathanael, who voiced skepticism (John 1:46) until he made his way to Jesus and talked with him. Then, Nathanael verbalized his discovery, saying, "Rabbi, thou art the Son of God; thou art the King of Israel" (John 1:49).

Here in school, you will find many academic gold nuggets, but remember it's the spiritual discoveries that will one day prove to be the most important.

Devotional focus:

In 1847, a doctor, Sir James Simpson, discovered chloroform, which made it possible for people to have surgeries without pain and suffering. The medical community called this finding one of the most significant in modern medicine. Dr. Simpson became a well-known lecturer at colleges and universities. One day during a question and answer session, someone asked, "What do you consider to be the most valuable discovery of your lifetime?" Everyone expected him to answer "chloroform," but Dr. Simpson said, "My most valuable discovery was when I discovered myself a sinner, and that Jesus Christ was my Savior". [1]

The Jewish nation had been waiting for the Messiah. When He arrived, most of the nation never really perceived it. A handful of people realized that the Messiah had been born. The church has experienced joy and peace through this wonderful discovery, which provides us with forgiveness, cleansing, restoration, and joy in knowing Jesus. Along with Dr. Simpson, may we joyfully say, "My most valuable discovery was when I realized I was a sinner, and that Jesus Christ was my Savior."

1. Paul Lee Tan, *Encyclopedia of 7700 Illustrations* (Chicago: R.R. Donnelly and Sons, Inc., 1979), 572.

Journal reflection:

____

____

____

____

____

____

____

____

____

An Invitation From the King

Scriptural insight:

. . . thou shalt eat bread at my table continually. (2 Samuel 9:7)

When David began his reign as the new king of Israel, he remembered his dear friend Jonathan. David had never forgotten that Jonathan had saved his life. With his friend dead, the new king sat in his palace and reflected on Jonathan's kindness and friendship. That's when he sent for a servant to ask if Jonathan had any descendants still living. He learned about Jonathan's son, a cripple, who lived in a barren place. David commanded the servant to bring him to the palace.

David met Mephibosheth and invited him to eat at his table continually. Jonathan's son felt undeserving, and he fell on his face, saying, "What is thy servant, that thou shouldest look upon such a dead dog as I am?" (2 Samuel 9:8). He may have felt unworthy, but the King wanted him at his table anyway. No doubt, strength, intelligence, and beauty characterized David's children, while the crippled Mephibosheth may have needed help or may have had to drag himself to the table. They had a blood tie to David, while Mephibosheth could claim no such relationship. The king, however, made him welcome, and he had the right to dine there. We often feel as Mephibosheth did, undeserving of the privilege, and certainly unworthy, of sitting at the King's table, but God welcomes us. The King of Kings has invited us to join Him at His table (Revelation 19:9).

Devotional focus:

When arriving on a college or university campus, we immediately begin interacting with other people, sharing a little of our history as we talk about our homes. We tell others a bit about our dream as we talk about the degree we have chosen and the career we have planned. While getting settled, we try to make friends and fit into the campus community. We may find, however, that the dorm we wanted has no place for us, ditto the campus club we wanted to join, and the classes offered at the right time. Other students may have filled all the spaces at the cafeteria table, even the seat beside a friend. We may find no room in the car carrying friends out for pizza. So, many times we feel like an outsider.

Musicians quickly make musician friends. Athletes swiftly make athletic friends. Virginians make friends from Virginia, while North or South Carolinians make friends with students from their states. We may soon learn, however, that we alone represent our neck of the woods and that no one else shares our particular interests. Then, we hear someone say, "This school is unfriendly." "No one seems to want to be my friend here." Students repeat these generalizations on school campuses across America.

What pains have you taken to make friends and become a part of campus life? These efforts require time and patience. If we feel a person or group has rebuffed us, we should move on to other people, clubs, classes, and, even, groups going for pizza. Refuse to be discouraged. Soon you will make friends who you will cherish for life. Just wait and see!

Journal reflection:

The Ultimate Textbook

Scriptural insight:

. . . the sword of the Spirit, which is the word of God. (Ephesians 6:17)

For the word of God is quick, and powerful, and sharper than any two-edged sword. (Hebrews 4:12)

For the prophecy came not in old time by the will of man: but holy men of God spake as they were moved by the Holy Ghost. (2 Peter 1:21)

Man shall not live by bread alone, but by every word that proceedeth out of the mouth of God. (Matthew 4:4)

Heaven and earth shall pass away, but my words shall not pass away. (Matthew 24:35)

At the first meeting of a class, you will usually receive a course syllabus that shows you what the class requires. Somewhere in the handout, you'll find a list of textbooks you must have for upcoming homework. You will first be surprised at the cost of these volumes, and then at how much time it takes to read the assignments. Many texts you study will influence your thoughts and ideas, for what you read does have a transforming effect upon you. Books that have horror stories may make you paranoid. Those that deal with self-esteem may give you more confidence. Texts that examine philosophy may make you more philosophical. Those that teach English and grammar may make you a better writer, while those that explore history may add to your knowledge about events of the past. The mind, though much more complex, resembles a computer in the way it stores what we see, hear, and read. With humans, however, the input may influence our actions. That's why we must choose carefully what materials we allow access to our minds.

To get a good education, we must read the Bible. In fact, teachers in the early days of our country used the Bible as a textbook. For example, a tour guide at Mount Vernon recently told us that Martha Washington used the Bible to teach her children to read. Our leaders founded our nation on its guiding principles. Over the centuries, however, people have banned, battled, and burned this Holy Book.

They have criticized, ridiculed, and rejected it. They have minimized and mocked its importance. Yet, students must realize the importance of the Bible. It tells us about the great love and mercy of God and how to receive the gift of eternal life. It tells us the eventual consequences and the fate of all who reject its message. It relates how to live a purposeful and successful life, and it foretells the future. It is a stabilizing and comforting force. It stands as the ultimate textbook.

Devotional focus:

I had heard that a person can read the Bible through in about 72 hours. So I decided to take the challenge. I even decided to finish the 66 books of the Bible in 66 days. I picked up the Bible on cassette, listening to some chapters as I drove. Other times, I read in the morning or afternoon. I averaged about an hour and 15 minutes a day listening and reading. Sure enough, I met my goal.

We issue a challenge to you. Rather than a 66-day assignment, we suggest that you discipline yourself to read the entire Bible. Most of you have great discipline. You need it to finish college courses, hobbies, work projects, and even difficult games. Some of you quickly finish a romance novel or sports book. Will you take the challenge to read and complete the ultimate textbook?

Journal reflection:

Student Aid

Scriptural insight:

But my God shall supply all your need according to his riches in glory by Christ Jesus. (Philippians 4:19)

God loves to answer the prayers of His children. He enjoys meeting our needs. He has the power to bring about incredible events in our lives. He has promised to supply whatever we need in life. Take the following incidents as examples:

- God gave Israel bread, water, and quail to satisfy the people's hunger and thirst.
- God delivered Israel in times of trouble.
- God provided a woman meal and oil to keep her from starving (1 Kings 17).
- God supplied a widow with oil to keep her family together (2 Kings 4).
- God multiplied bread and fish to feed 5,000 hungry people (Matthew 14).
- God presented Simon with tax money when it was due (Matthew 17).

The pages of God's Word record many incredible miracles that God has given to His children. He encourages us to ask, seek, and knock (Matthew 7:7-11). He takes great pleasure in meeting our needs. He does, however, meet those needs in His own time and in His perfect way. I'm delighted that He chose to disregard some of my prayers, delayed answering others, and responded to many in unexpected ways. Most of all, I'm thankful that He meets our needs.

Devotional focus:

Stories of the journeys and struggles of others often give us strength. Knowing that someone else has survived difficult situations encourages us. Hearing what God has done for another person in need also builds our faith. Take the following story, for example.

A young man arrived at Lee University and quickly felt at home in the special atmosphere that southern hospitality creates. He did occasionally feel homesick and made the 200-mile trip to his home as often as he could. A severe shortage of money, however, marked his most difficult obstacle, and his family lacked the means to help him. One semester he found himself with only 17 cents to his name. Without access to the food bill, he checked with the student aid office for funds. He learned that the office could provide him no more money for loans, and that no grants were available. He had a great financial need, so he prayed a desperate prayer that God would give him a miracle. He felt directed to return to the financial aid office again. As he entered the room to request assistance, a man entered at about the same time. He said, "I'm a painter, and I've just had someone quit. I need someone to hold a ladder for me for a few minutes. I'll pay them $15.00." The student spoke up and said, "Sir, I'll be glad to help you." He held the ladder while the man finished the job. The painter handed him $15.00. This money bought some food for a hungry student.

The financial aid office serves as a lifesaver for many. Being given the money to survive another semester really takes the pressure off students who have little support. But you'll find the ultimate student aid office above. You will need no appointment. God has your best interest at heart and will provide an answer. He certainly has the assets for those who will submit a request through a prayer of faith.

Journal reflection:

My Guidance Counselor

Scriptural insight:

For unto us a child is born, unto us a son is given: and the government shall be upon his shoulder: and his name shall be called Wonderful, Counsellor, The mighty God, The everlasting Father, The Prince of Peace. (Isaiah 9:6)

Howbeit when he, the Spirit of truth, is come, he will guide you into all truth. (John 16:13)

Knowing the right decisions to make at certain times in our lives can present a challenge. Choosing the best path in the face of so many options may be distressing. Sometimes taking the direction that appears most attractive turns out to be a wonderful choice. At other times, however, that option brings horrible consequences. Often, the decision to take a less-traveled path or to make an unpopular choice proves to be perfect for us. Many friends have told me about times when they desperately needed to know which way to go. For example, one young man received an offer for a wonderful position with a good salary, but he prayed for guidance and had a strong inclination to decline the position. Later, he realized why. That decision would have sent him along a totally different route for his life. The "no" he received in prayer and his obedience to follow that direction eventually led him to greater opportunities.

The Bible describes the Lord as "a wonderful counselor," and it tells us that the Holy Spirit wants to guide us in the right way. We must of necessity spend time in prayerful reflection about the many decisions that face us in life. Sometimes we fail to see or understand where our decisions will lead us, but we can trust the Lord, knowing that He will make the best choices for us. He will guide us, if we will pray, listen, and obediently pursue the direction that He has revealed.

Devotional focus:

The following story from a student may help you face some of the difficult decisions you must make. This young man had reached a crossroad. He had an opportunity to attend an outstanding school, yet he felt hesitant that the school offered the right path for his life. He sought counsel from several people and listened intently to their comments as they advised him that school would be the right decision. Still undecided, he decided to seek spiritual direction. He was determined to receive the Lord's guidance. Even so, the first day of classes rolled around, and he waited for an answer to his prayers. He decided to attend class the first day. He walked toward the building with great uncertainty, but, as he entered the building, an overwhelming sense of peace enveloped him. That assurance settled his mind, and he was able to confidently pursue an education. He graduated with his degree, and a great door of opportunity opened for his career. The timing could not have been more perfect.

You'll no doubt meet good guidance counselors and some who seem disinterested in your fate. The guidance we receive from above, however, will always be in our best interest, will always be correct. This student still has his guidance counselor with him, with an appointment to talk to Him only a prayer away.

Journal reflection:

____

____

____

____

____

____

____

____

____

Your Father Knows

Scriptural insight:

Are not five sparrows sold for two farthings, and not one of them is forgotten before God? But even the very hairs of your head are all numbered. Fear not therefore: ye are of more value than many sparrows. (Luke 12:6-7)

But he knoweth the way that I take. (Job 23:10)

Lord, thou knowest all things. (John 21:17)

In the last few years, most states have begun requiring high school students to pass a test before graduation. The state of Virginia requires students to pass the SOL test. Tennessee requires students to pass the TACAP. To get into college or university, students usually must take the SAT or the ACT, College Board entrance tests that cause great stress for high school seniors. These test scores reveal a student's educational standing. The results determine which colleges or universities will accept a potential student.

After receiving a bachelor's or master's degree, you'd think you would be finished with exams. However, many companies require you to complete a test before they'll offer you a job. All these examinations reveal the level of knowledge a person possesses. Tests actually show how much information a person can recall. When referring to the ability to recall information, psychologists talk about our neuron cells. These brain cells amass vast amounts of knowledge and control our bodies. Computer companies talk about RAM, which refers to how much data a computer holds. Game shows have large viewing audiences because viewers want to see if contestants can answer certain questions. When it comes to knowledge and storing information, we should recognize our limitations. We've all felt pretty dumb while watching brilliant contestants answer hard questions on Jeopardy.

The Bible speaks about God's knowledge and ability to recall information. He has unlimited knowledge. We learn that He knows the number of hairs on our heads. Years ago in Palestine, vendors sold sparrows for food. When a person would buy four sparrows, the fifth one would be thrown in for good measure. Luke tells us that God even remembers that fifth sparrow. This informs us that He knows our location, and He knows about all our problems. Like David, we may be tempted to say, "Such knowledge is too wonderful for me" (Psalm 139:6). Not only wonderful, but it is also comforting. By the way, God chooses to forget one thing. Can you name it? (Hebrews 10:17)

Devotional focus:

Some recent technological breakthroughs amaze us. Take, for example, a Global Positioning System that tracks people, vehicles, and animals. My neighbor had access to a satellite. He once watched his brother place hamburgers on a grill in another state. He called his brother on the phone and surprised him by telling him what color shirt he was wearing.

As we prepared to sign the mortgage on our home, I thought no one noticed my apprehension. Borrowing such a large sum of money almost paralyzed me with fear. Suddenly, about two feet from my face, a sparrow hovered in the window with no sign of a branch for landing. The bird had no reason to stop in midair, and it stayed in one spot for about twenty seconds. I took this as a sign that God wanted me to know that I should not worry. So I smiled and signed the papers. We've made every mortgage payment on time. God's knowledge of us works better than any GPS. He does provide for every sparrow, and He does know everything about us (Matthew 6:26).

You may have a cold, face a test, or feel disappointed, lonely, or fearful. Maybe you have called home or e-mailed your family many times in similar situations. This time, however, you have either chosen not to call or have been unable to reach them. You feel all alone and wish your family knew about your difficulty. Your family may not know, but your Heavenly Father does.

Journal reflection:

____

____

____

How Big Is Your God?

Scriptural insight:

. . . wherefore hast thou stolen my gods? (Genesis 31:30)

Now Rachel had taken the images, and put them in the camel's furniture, and sat upon them. (Genesis 31:34)

To whom then will ye liken God? Or what likeness will ye compare unto him? (Isaiah 40:18)

Many dramas fill the book of Genesis. For example, one story tells of Jacob fleeing with his family from Laban. Jacob had worked for Laban for 20 years, and God had greatly blessed him. During that time, he had established a family and gathered many herds of animals. Sensing that Laban resented his blessings, Jacob left, as quietly as possible, with his family and herds, but Rachel took the gods of Laban and hid them beneath her camel's saddle. No one detected these gods, although they searched for them. Laban pursued them, and the drama concludes with God protecting Jacob and his family.

When we hear about the small size of Laban's gods, we wonder about some of the gods that others worship. Throughout history, man has made tens of thousands of gods (Acts 17), creating them from gold, silver, brass, stone, and wood (Revelation 9:20). People have worshiped the sun, moon, and stars, as well as insects and animals. They have worshiped another person and even, in one situation, a tooth that they believed to be holy.

Isaiah echoed a question from God to man in Isaiah 40. God asked to whom we would compare Him. That chapter talks about God's greatness. Unlike Laban's idols, God would never fit beneath a saddle. We need never ring a bell to awaken Him, nor chain Him up at night to protect Him from thieves, nor guard Him from those who would try to destroy Him. Greater than the universe (1 Kings 8:27), He made Himself small enough to fit in a manger (Luke 2:7; Isaiah 7:14). Somehow God can even live in a person's heart (John 14:23).

Devotional focus:

Many challenges will face every student pursuing a degree. You will experience highs and lows. You may have faith and optimism, as well as doubts and discouragement. Handling good times will be easy, while dealing with challenges will be hard. Having a strong faith in God will be vital to your survival and success. We titled this devotional "How Big is Your God?" to help you focus upon where you have placed your faith. Let me ask you some important questions about your faith in God.

- Is your God big enough to have a plan and destiny for your life?
- Does your God know where you have come from, and can He forgive you for your sins and failures?
- Can your God meet your needs and hear you when you pray?
- Will your God strengthen you when you are weak?
- Has your God comforted and calmed you during troublesome times?

A New York City taxi driver picked up a Christian. As they made their way through the city, the Christian noticed several small images on the dashboard. When asked what they were, the man said that they were his gods. They were so small that they could fit on his dashboard. How big is your God?

Journal reflection:

____

____

____

____

____

Chapter Twelve

The Pursuit of Happiness

1. *Trivial Pursuit*
2. *Have You Ever Been in a Cave?*
3. *The Problem Class*
4. *The Investment of a Lifetime*
5. *How to Enjoy the Journey*
6. *Inside-Out Happiness*
7. *Get Over It!*

Voices and Choices

"One of the biggest mistakes that I made was not staying in touch with my family. Talking to my family has always encouraged me."

"I stayed in my room too much. If I had gotten out more and gotten more involved, then I believe I would have been happier."

"My advice is to find a place to fit in. Don't be so isolated."

"I didn't know that there were so many parks and fun places near my university. If I had known about them when I was going to school, it would have helped a lot."

Journal Focus

Have you ever felt discouraged and wondered why? Have you wondered what you could do to lift your spirits? Writing about discouragement and about how to overcome it seems to help. This week, why not journal some of your thoughts about depression and happiness?

Strength Through Prayer

"Dear Lord, You know me better than anyone else. You see me when I'm confident and encouraged. You also see me when I'm filled with doubts and discouragement. Please lead me from times of discouragement into greater happiness and fulfillment. In Jesus name I pray. Amen."

Trivial Pursuit

Scriptural insight:

After whom is the king of Israel come out? after whom dost thou pursue? after a dead dog, after a flea. (1 Samuel 24:14)

Now therefore, let not my blood fall to the earth before the face of the Lord: for the king of Israel is come out to seek a flea, as when one doth hunt a partridge in the mountains. (1 Samuel 26:20)

Saul, the king of Israel, had achieved great success. He had been firmly established as the first king of Israel. Militarily, he had experienced great victories against his enemies. Monetarily, he had great possessions and wealth. Personally, he had a wonderful family that lived with him in his palace. As status goes, he ranked number one in the success department. So why, you may wonder, did he choose to stumble along in the darkness with several thousand choice soldiers rather than to stay at home enjoying his family, success, and fame? Why did Saul find relaxing and enjoying his life so difficult? What drove him so insistently?

For the answers, we must go back in time. Following the defeat of Goliath and the Philistines, the women of Jerusalem sang a song about their leaders. They ascribed the greatest victory to David, and gave David more acclaim than they did the king. The song struck a sour note in Saul's heart, filling him with jealousy. The relationship between Saul and David deteriorated. Saul sought to end David's life. In the next scene, Saul and his soldiers stumbled along in the darkness chasing David. The voice of David pierced the night on two occasions. David asked Saul why he would chase a dead dog and a flea. David, an ally of Saul's, firmly supported his king. He had no wish to hurt him. Rather, he wanted to do what he could to help him. So David summed it up, telling Saul it was as if he chased a dead dog or a flea. This man with all his great power chose to pursue someone insignificant. We may learn a great lesson from this example. What do we pursue, and why do we pursue it? Is it, as David said, like a dead dog or a flea?

Devotional focus:

Families with this problem may be embarrassed. They try to keep it a secret, but the secret is out when you're visiting and a flea crawls across your hand. As you survey the room and see their pet dog or cat, you know the source of the problem. To avoid embarrassing them, you quietly try to finish off the flea. Fleas, however, move fast and fight to the finish.

You might say that comparing the priorities of one's life to chasing a dead dog or pursuing a flea ranks as a tragedy. I often find myself amazed and shocked at what I see and hear. Scores of people pursue dead dogs and fleas. I've heard people recount how many years it has taken them to collect inconsequential and trivial items. Others tell of spending a lifetime building an object or trying to reach a goal that has no real relevance or purpose. For instance, building sand castles may be fun and must have some artistic value, but a surging tide quickly washes away a whole day's work.

I hope that none of us behave like King Saul, who was guilty of neglecting his family, wasting his time, ill appreciating his successes, and making the insignificant his main concern. Students must closely monitor how they spend their time, regularly questioning their priorities. They must think about what they are pursuing. The game Trivial Pursuit may be fun to play. We should not, however, let it be a game that defines how we spend our lives.

Journal reflection:

____

____

____

____

____

____

Have You Ever Been in a Cave?

Scriptural insight:

And he arose, and did eat and drink, and went in the strength of that meat forty days and forty nights unto Horeb the mount of God. And he came thither unto a cave, and lodged there; and, behold, the word of the Lord came to him, and he said unto him, What doest thou here, Elijah? (1 Kings 19:8-9)

When it comes to dedication and striving to serve God, few men surpass Elijah (1 Kings 19:14). The pages of God's Word reveal that as a prophet, he continually performed his ministry with excellence. We witness God answering Elijah's marvelous prayers and giving him miracles, and we see Elijah working with what seemed to be tireless energy. Suddenly, though, Elijah seemed to hit a wall emotionally, seemed to have gone as far as he could go. He even prayed that God would take his life (I Kings 19:4). I doubt that this prayer represented his true feelings. Had he wanted to die, he could have stayed put, and Jezebel would have had him killed (1 Kings 19:2-3). I'm glad that God leaves some of our prayers unanswered!

A depressed and exhausted prophet enters a cave to isolate himself from others and preserve his life. He seems almost to resign his prophetic office. As he sits in the cave, the Lord suddenly speaks to him, wanting to know what he's doing there. God already knew the answer. God wanted Elijah to do a little reflecting upon his depressed condition. It's good, occasionally, to take a close look at ourselves.

The Lord told the prophet to get out of the cave and stand on the mountain (1 Kings 19:11). God gave some visible signs that showed His great power (1 Kings 19:11-12). God then spoke in a still small voice to this depressed man (I1 Kings 19:12). He reminded Elijah that he was not alone, and God gave him new direction (1 Kings 19:15-18). Elijah emerged from his cave of depression with renewed strength to accomplish his new assignments. God took Elijah from a cave of depression and accomplished His purposes through him.

Devotional focus:

I love to visit caverns. The Lost Sea Cavern was one of the first caverns I visited, and certainly stands as the most interesting. Located in East Tennessee, near Sweetwater, this underground lake contains more than 13 acres of water. A glass bottom boat carried me for a ride, while huge trout swam below.

I remember the Indian Echo Cavern in Hershey, Pennsylvania, as the most surprising. It grabs your interest because, years ago, a man named Amos Wilson lived in that cave for 19 years. He died there, and somebody eventually found his body. People called him "The Pennsylvania Hermit." I asked about his tragic story and learned that his sister had been influenced to commit a crime, for which the courts sentenced her to hang. Amos made his way to the governor, throwing himself at the official's feet and begging for mercy. The governor wrote a pardon. As Amos made his way back to rescue his sister, a heavy rain caused the river to rise, preventing him from crossing for several hours. When he finally arrived at the place of execution, they had just hanged his sister. This event caused Amos to withdraw and to live in a cave until he died.

I would describe caves—with their darkness, isolation, and walls that seem to close in on you—as depressing places. A visit may be interesting, but to live there would be a tragedy. I've met many people who live in another kind of cave. Like Elijah, they enter a cave because they have been disheartened, disappointed, or disillusioned. Like Amos Wilson, life has deeply wounded them. Coping with their pain seems to be out of the question.

I'm thankful that God worked in the life of Elijah. No one had to discover his body in a cave. He came forth from his cave of depression and resumed a life of significance and purpose. Have you ever been in a cave? I certainly have, but I have chosen to leave there, to recover from my hurts, and to strive to achieve a life of significance and purpose. How about you?

Journal reflection:

The Problem Class

Scriptural insight:

Yet man is born unto trouble, as the sparks fly upward. (Job 5:7)

Man that is born of a woman is of few days, and full of trouble. (Job 14:1)

Many are the afflictions of the righteous: but the Lord delivereth him out of them all. (Psalm 34:19)

The words "trouble" and "affliction" bring images of suffering. These words quickly transport us mentally to some unpleasant places in our minds. We can all remember personal struggles and our most painful memories. Thoughts of money problems, family problems, and health problems readily come to mind. We can recall tragedies that have struck on high school, college, and university campuses. Students never forget the memorial service of a close friend, and they easily call up mental images from newscasts about events on campuses throughout America.

In the course of a lifetime, everyone will experience such dreadful places that fill us with questions and emotions. I should know; my best friend and college roommate died suddenly one night. I doubted that I could survive at that terrible moment. When a crisis arrives, people often recognize the importance of prayer. When trouble comes, people remember to look up for divine assistance, and they also find loving friends and a supportive community. Only in the midst of hard times can you discover your real friends.

The Bible tells us that He walks with us in times of trouble (Psalm 138:7) and as we journey through the deepest valleys (Psalm 23:4). He promises that His divine presence will never leave us (Matthew 28:20).

Devotional focus:

The class focused on trouble or, more specifically, on how to handle trouble. One night, the class amazed me with its response to the professor's question. When he asked, "How many of you have trouble?" everyone in the class raised a hand. This made such a strong impression upon me that I counted the number of class members. I carefully looked over these 55 students composed of mostly successful community leaders. The parking lot revealed that they drove new and expensive cars. They held important positions. How could they all have difficulties? At my young age, I sat there trying to process their response. I had reasoned that, at their age, success and wealth would solve most problems. These leaders had both success and wealth, but they also had trouble.

Twenty-five years after graduation, I can still remember vividly that problem class. Life has taught me that everyone will face trials regardless of social status. I've learned that trouble can become a potential pitfall, if we face it in the wrong way. I have also learned what to do in the midst of tribulations. I must seek the Lord in prayer to receive the strength necessary to endure and survive. I'm sorry to tell you that difficulty will eventually come your way. I'm not wishing it upon you. I'm simply stating a fact. When it does come, what will you do and how will you survive? Remember to read God's Word, to pray, and to let the community around you strengthen you.

Journal reflection:

The Investment of a Lifetime

Scriptural insight:

And the younger of them said to his father, Father, give me the portion of goods that falleth to me. And he divided unto him his living. And not many days after the younger son gathered all together, and took his journey into a far country, and there wasted his substance with riotous living. (Luke 15:12-13)

There was a certain rich man, which had a steward; and the same was accused unto him that he had wasted his goods. (Luke 16:1)

No one wants to be guilty of wasting money. After all, it takes work to gain money, and it takes money to do most anything. For instance, a walk though one of our local parks cost you $4, and a drive down a scenic road at a state park costs you $15. We pay for many items and services to survive, making us wonder how our money disappears so fast. Most of us know how much we have in our checkbook and how many bills we have coming due, so we must use wisdom about our budget and purchases.

Few people receive large amounts of money through an inheritance or investment. An exception would be the young man of Jesus' parable. He asked his successful father for his inheritance, and his dad gave him a large sum of money. The son quickly packed and escaped from his home. He reveled in his newfound freedom. He spent his money on new friends, but he soon discovered that these friends disappeared when he had spent all his inheritance. He sought employment in the swine industry.

The steward in another of Jesus' parables also had a problem with handling money. A rich man entrusted him to invest some money. He must have used poor judgment about investment opportunities. Before long, he had wasted the money and quickly tried to salvage his future.

These examples might remind us of some of our decisions. Have you ever wanted to kick yourself for buying an item you could do without? Wasting money makes us feel foolish; however, God has given us something more precious to spend than money. He has given us an allotted amount of time, and spending it wisely will prove to be our greatest investment.

Devotional focus:

We occasionally saw him out in his yard, where he rarely stood on his feet. Many times, we would drive along and see him stumbling or even sprawled out on the lawn. I'm talking about a man who lived in our neighborhood many years ago. By his 30s, he already walked with a cane. In his early 40s when I met him, he had spent his whole life chasing the high that comes from alcohol. Our encounter left me feeling sad. I could see that he had had great potential and wondered what he could have become had he only applied himself. A short time later, I learned that he had died. Some may consider a drunken high funny. I wish everyone pursuing alcohol could see how they might turn out if they continue down that path. This precious man mismanaged his time, and wasted his life.

People often ask students about time management. They may ask, "You aren't wasting all your time, are you?" Paul discussed his time expenditure, saying, "And I will very gladly spend and be spent for you" (2 Corinthians 12:15). He wanted the church to know that he used his time trying to establish the early church because he loved them. His passion motivated him to serve God. Giving himself to the purpose for his life completed and fulfilled him.

Scores of college students invest their time in activities that pay awful dividends. Drive by a college after midnight, and you may see some of them passed out on the lawn. You may have seen their crumpled vehicle on the news. You may have visited them in a hospital, or you may even have wept at their funeral. We have witnessed the results of many tragedies following a night of partying. The path you take will certainly lead you somewhere. The decisions you make will have some consequences.

How are you investing the time that God has allotted you? Will you invest your life in important endeavors? Will you give yourself to purposes worthy of your life? Students must give themselves to books instead of booze, study instead of sex, and discipline instead of drugs. How are you investing your life?

Journal reflection:

How to Enjoy the Journey

Scriptural insight:

Not that I speak in respect of want: for I have learned, in whatsoever state I am, therewith to be content. (Philippians 4:11)

Let your conversation be without covetousness; and be content with such things as ye have: for he hath said, I will never leave thee, nor forsake thee. (Hebrews 13:5)

If there has ever been a person that should have been discouraged, it was Paul. He experienced spiritual and physical problems that we could never relate to. In spite of these crushing challenges, he had learned to be content.

Paul advises us that we can be happy and satisfied even under the most difficult of circumstances. At one point in his life, Paul could have been executed at any time. Yet, he rose above sad and difficult conditions to live a contented life no matter the situation.

This is a lesson that we all must learn. Sometimes gloom so envelops our lives that even finding a warm smile for a friend requires too much of us. Our faces often reflect our stress, doubt, and misery. Our tears or bad attitude may reveal our discontent. We all know that people differ. While some can handle loads of pressure, others stress out over the slightest challenge. Some show a happy countenance under the most adverse condition; others appear depressed in even the best of times. While life's pull and tug may prevent our living on a mountain and being happy all the time, neither should we stay in a valley that perpetuates sadness. Have you ever taken the time to monitor your moods? Do you find the stress that brings sadness and discontentment really worth such a terrible response? What can you do to control your emotions when events go wrong?

Devotional focus:

Pig Pen is a very interesting *Peanuts* character. A cloud of dirt follows him everywhere he goes. It seems to hover over him, along with the unsuspecting people he meets. Once aware, they quickly try to escape. Pig Pen reminds me of many people I've met. Instead of dirt, their cover consists of discontentment. Most people quickly excuse themselves from the presence of someone like Pig Pen and try to find someone who offers a ray of sunshine.

How can we enjoy the journey through school? What can we do to make a gloomy cloud dissipate? These helpful questions will challenge you to make a paradigm shift:

- Do you attend such campus activities as concerts or plays?
- Have you been to mixers or gatherings offered to help you?
- Have you challenged a friend to a ping-pong match?
- Do you support the baseball, softball, soccer, football, or basketball teams?
- Have you tried to meet new friends?
- Are you grateful for your educational opportunities?
- Have you read a book that offers humor or encouragement?
- Have you walked around campus and admired its beauty?
- Could you list 10 reasons why a student should be happy and contented?

A senior driving four other college students one day found amazing all their negative comments. Later, one student would become a doctor; another, a pharmacist; and the other two, public school teachers. All four had a cloud over them, as they talked about the terrible food, professors, and classes. Even so, all four have become successful. Now, they look back and see everything they endured in a different, positive light. They would tell you to enjoy your journey and to avoid falling into a rut of negativity.

Journal reflection:

____

____

____

____

Inside-Out Happiness

Scriptural insight:

. . . and I therein do rejoice, yea, and will rejoice. (Philippians 1:18)

Finally, my brethren, rejoice in the Lord. (Philippians 3:1)

Rejoice in the Lord always: and again I say, Rejoice. (Philippians 4:4)

But I rejoiced in the Lord greatly. (Philippians 4:10)

One of the mysteries of life lies in how differently people perceive and react to circumstances around them. Take the apostle Paul for example. He had endured great suffering as he labored for the Lord. He had experienced many hardships that nearly claimed his life. He finally found himself a prisoner in Rome. For several years, he had anticipated his approaching death, as his letters reflect. Yet, in the midst of his lost freedom and impending death, he had great tranquility and began to make converts out of some of the soldiers who guarded him. He rejoiced even in his dreary state. Had he lost his touch with reality? Did he understand what the future held? How could a prisoner on deathwatch be so happy? These questions reveal an important truth for us.

He refused to let his mind dwell on the negative circumstances of his situation. He set his mind upon spiritual matters, passionately seeking to do his best, finish his race, and keep the faith (2 Timothy 4:6-8). So, it appears, Paul's true happiness and joy came not from his situation, but from above. Neither should our circumstances determine our happiness and joy.

Devotional focus:

On a normal day as I went about my routine duties, I met an old man in a nursing home whom I have never forgotten. He had been confined to a bed for many years. His words have come to my mind often when I have felt discomfort and dissatisfaction. He smiled and said, "I have been in this nursing home for 11 years. I'm very thankful. These people take good care of me." He showed no sign of anger, pessimism, or depression. Like Paul, he had something on the inside. Despite his declining health, impending death, lack of mobility, and total dependence upon others, he had happiness and joy. On routine days on many campuses across America, you will meet people like these two men. You will also meet people who show their pessimistic nature. Sit with them in the cafeteria, and you know they will soon serve up some complaint about the food, the professors, and a host of other subjects. Obviously, their crankiness stems from more than their present challenges.

If you find yourself persistently negative, take a close look at your life. What changes do you need to make to enjoy your gift of life? Can you notice the positive side of matters and share some affirmative thoughts with others? Pessimistic people bring others down. They will fill you with despair. Optimistic people lift others up. We all face bad days, but the good days far outweigh them any time. Happiness and joy do come from within, not from your circumstances. Look on the bright side!

Journal reflection:

Get Over It!

Scriptural insight:

For by thee I have run through a troop: by my God have I leaped over a wall. (2 Samuel 22:30)

David faced more hardship and opposition than most people will ever face. He faced and slew a bear and a lion. He suffered his brothers' scorn and verbal abuse. He took down a giant for his country. He endured King Saul's hatred. He twice escaped death from a javelin. He tolerated the king's treating him like a criminal. He bore his father-in-law giving his wife to another man. Lonely, cold, hungry, and bewildered, he shed lots of tears and had many questions. His friend betrayed him; his son conspired against him. His family scandalized him, and he even saw the death of several of his children. Yet, through it all, the Bible shows us that God stood with him. David eventually rose above all of his difficult times. He joyfully said, "I have run through a troop; by my God have I leaped over a wall." In other words, he jumped over his obstacles. One could say that he got over it!

Many times, we suffer incidents that seem impossible to overcome. I often think of an Old Testament family that had to overcome a painful situation. I doubt that most people would remember the family name, Korah. Like the names Judas or Benedict Arnold, Korah ranks right up there with objectionable names. You'll find Korah's dreadful story in Numbers 16. This chapter tells us about a rebellion that Korah instigated against Moses. The rebellion led to the ground suddenly opening up and swallowing Korah and some of his friends. As the ground came back together, it buried them alive. The sons of Korah, no doubt, saw their father and his friends die. I wonder if they felt angry with God. I wonder if some people ostracized them. I wonder if they had to work hard to regain the respect of others. How could they ever live down this terrible shame against their family name? Amazingly, the Bible dedicates 11 chapters of Psalms to the sons of Korah. His descendants actively worked in ministry. They refused to let their father's failure hamper them from succeeding. They got over it and moved on with their lives to become important in temple ministry.

Devotional focus:

I've often heard people discuss how difficult they find overcoming some incidents. Well, history tells us that David got over it. History also records that Joseph, the sons of Korah, and many others got over being hurt. You, too, can get over the deep hurts and disappointments of life, whether they stem from your decisions and failures or from the actions of others. Whatever the source of your pain, God can restore you.

Driving along Interstate 66 on June 14, 2007, I listened to a syndicated radio program that took phone calls from across the nation and played dedications and requests for listeners. A woman called to relay an inspirational story of resilience. Pregnant at age 16, she found herself on her own with a child at 17. A little later, she married and had two other children. Her lifelong dream had been to pursue a nursing degree. Now at 34 years of age, she said that she had just graduated from a nursing program with honors. She had refused to let her past failures and mistakes affect her. She got over her failures and mistakes.

Have you ever heard anyone make comments such as these: "He'll never get over it." "I can't get over being hurt so badly." "I can't get over the way I was treated." "I can't get over the bad feelings I have against them." We have all heard people relive a terrible and painful moment and express grave doubt about ever being the same person again. For all those who have painful memories, let us share some practical thoughts about the process of restoration. To get past the hurt:

- You must want to get past it.
- You must refuse to continue to relive it mentally, or talk about it verbally.
- You must forgive others.
- You must forgive yourself.
- You may need to talk to others who have conquered a similar situation.

- You must realize that healing a deep wound often takes a lot of time.

You may feel you've been scandalized, victimized, ostracized, or traumatized, but God still heals and restores. So, Get Over It!

Journal reflection:

Chapter Thirteen

The Courage to Continue

1. *Don't Let Anyone Bury Your Dreams*
2. *A Trip to the Gym*
3. *Lessons From the Ant*
4. *Marching Through the Poop*
5. *Beat the Odds*
6. *The Holding Pattern*
7. *Fitting In Without Fading Out*

Voices and Choices

"I found a student-led discussion group. That helped me a lot."

"I have been very lonely. I was popular back home. It takes a while to adjust."

"Everyone feels like quitting sometime. I'm glad I didn't give in to that temptation."

"All of us get homesick. We have to keep on going in spite of our feelings."

"The Lord gave me the strength and courage I needed to finish my education."

Journal Focus

We all recognize the difficulty in pursuing an education. The process does require lots of patience. Can you reflect upon some times that you have exhibited daring in the face of difficulty? Write some thoughts in your journal about having the courage to endure.

Strength Through Prayer

"Dear Lord, You know me better than anyone else. You see me when I'm confident and encouraged. You also see me when I'm filled with doubts and discouragement. Please lead me from times of discouragement and give me the courage I need to continue. Amen."

Don't Let Anyone Bury Your Dreams

Scriptural insight:

For all the wells which his father's servants had digged in the days of Abraham his father, the Philistines had stopped them, and filled them with earth. (Genesis 26:15)

And Isaac digged again the wells of water, which they had digged in the days of Abraham his father. (Genesis 26:18)

In Palestine, where the land lies dry and barren in many places, the people value water as an extremely precious and scarce commodity. In our country, where we simply turn a faucet and the water begins to flow, we hardly know how to relate to such dry conditions.

Genesis tells us that Isaac needed water for his family and his herds, so he decided to dig again the wells that his father had once dug. Over the years, enemies had filled in the wells with dirt. In fact, during an enemy attack, the soldiers would try to cut off the water supply, as well as cut down or burn fruit trees, grapevines, and crops. When Isaac's servants dug in one of his father's old wells, they found water, but soon a neighbor claimed the well and took it away from them. They repeated the process only to have a neighbor take that one away too. These setbacks could have caused Isaac to give up, but he refused to quit. Dirt in the wells could not hinder him, nor would the wells being taken away discourage him. He refused to stop short of accomplishing his goal of having water, even though he faced difficult and trying circumstances. His dream finally became a reality.

Devotional focus:

Many people around us must have descended from the Philistines. They want to oppose, resist, and bury the well that could be called your dreams. They stand ready to throw the dirt of criticism and doubt as you talk about doing something wonderful with your life. As you dream of pursuing a career or talk about what you want to accomplish, you can almost see the shovel in their hands. If you want to attend a college or university, they will probably point out how much it costs. They may tell you of the difficulties you will face. They may tell a horror story about someone who failed or had a bad experience.

Isaac could have allowed those who opposed him to put an end to his efforts, but he realized the water's importance. He refused to let dirt cover or bury his dream or to let his feelings of being treated unjustly stop him from having a dream. He exhibited a fierce tenacity about digging. Though circumstances may have been discouraging, he continued to dig until he found success.

You should expect someone at some point to throw dirt upon your dream, and you may also have someone treat you unfairly. To be successful, you will have to exhibit a fierce tenacity if you want to accomplish your dreams. Discouraging times may come, but refuse to let anyone bury your dreams. Dare to be a dreamer, and strive to accomplish your dreams until they become a reality.

Journal reflection:

A Trip to the Gym

Scriptural insight:

. . . and exercise thyself rather unto godliness. For bodily exercise profiteth little: but godliness is profitable unto all things, having promise of the life that now is, and of that which is to come. (1 Timothy 4:7-8)

But I keep under my body, and bring it into subjection: lest that by any means, when I have preached to others, I myself should be a castaway. (1 Corinthians 9:27)

Paul must have loved sporting events, for they seemed to be on his mind quite often as he wrote his letters. If Paul lived today, he would probably have a favorite team and watch ESPN. We see him using several metaphors about racing, wrestling, and fighting. When Paul talked about exercise and discipline, he used the Greek word "gumnazo," which refers to going to a gymnasium to exercise.[1] Avid sportsmen and those who love to stay in shape may take offense at some of Paul's words, as he seems to downplay exercise. Paul realized that staying in shape spiritually was a much greater priority than physical exercise. A man or woman may have a great physique, but let their spiritual muscle turn to flab. So Paul talked about keeping himself in shape spiritually, fearing that his lack of discipline could affect his relationship with God. He also encouraged Timothy to pursue a spiritual exercise program.

Devotional focus:

You can see a difference between people who exercise and those who skip it. People who stay in shape often talk of being buff and having hard pecs, references to a body in excellent shape. They take pride in having toned muscles. We often see them leaving the gym with a workout bag containing their sweaty clothes. They have pushed themselves once again, determined to keep themselves in top physical condition. Others rarely exercise. They may have the desire, but they let their busy schedules come before a workout commitment. Some have small children and get exercise trying to keep up with them. Many recognize their need to get into shape but may feel others have rebuffed them for not being buff. Many of us have pecs buried way beneath—well, I'll stop right there. Many of us feel almost embarrassed to go to a gym. The sight of all those toned bodies can be humiliating; the weight room and treadmills, intimidating. Realizing our dilemma, lots of us have taken to walking and working out on our own.

Teachers and professors use the word "exercise" in a different manner, referring to a project, test, or class assignment. Just as we require training to keep our bodies and spirits in shape, we need training to develop our minds. Great athletes push themselves. People with great minds must push themselves too. You will never be spiritually developed unless you exercise spiritually. You will never be physically conditioned unless you exercise physically. You will never be a successful student unless you exercise mentally. I'm talking about reading the chapters the professor has assigned, disciplining yourself to study, and completing required research papers and projects. Preparing oneself mentally does take exercise. Are you applying yourself mentally? Are you spending time in the gym?

1. James Strong, *Strong's Exhaustive Concordance of the Bible* (Peabody, MA: Hendrickson Publishers, 1890), 325.

Journal reflection:

____

____

____

____

____

____

____

Lessons From the Ant

Scriptural insight:

Go to the ant, thou sluggard; consider her ways, and be wise: Which having no guide, overseer, or ruler, Provideth her meat in the summer, and gathereth her food in the harvest. (Proverbs 6:6-8)

The ants are a people not strong, yet they prepare their meat in the summer. (Proverbs 30:25)

The Lord spoke to Jeremiah, directing him to go to the potter's house (Jeremiah 18). He told Elijah to exit a cave and observe nature (1 Kings 19). He instructed Moses to throw his staff down and stick his hand into his clothing (Exodus 4). In all three cases, following God's directive taught the men a lesson. We can gain knowledge of significance without seeking out renowned scholars or the world's best thinkers. Solomon pointed us to an unlikely source, the minute ant, to gain wisdom. These tiny insects can ruin a picnic, they can move an elephant, and they can teach vital lessons about life.

While small, an ant can accomplish mighty feats. Some barely cover the head of a pin, and others measure the length of a thumbnail. Yet, they gather, carry, and store enough food to preserve their colony through the winter. The ant persists. Someone once counted the times that an ant tried to carry a crumb up a wall. It failed more than 50 times before finally prevailing and hauling that crumb to the top. We can learn some huge lessons from some tiny teachers.

Devotional focus:

A graduate shared his story of how difficult achieving success had been for him. His family provided little tuition help, so he had to handle the bulk of his college expenses. An opportunity for weekend employment came his way. The job would pay well, but he would be required to drive about 200 miles one way to work. So from Monday morning through Friday afternoon he went to class and studied. Then from Friday afternoon through Sunday midnight, he labored in a factory. In addition, he devoted his Sunday mornings to his local church as a musician. For four years, he pursued these three endeavors, studying, laboring, and playing music. Finally, he graduated and today has become an extremely successful leader.

One morning, as I worked in a factory, my supervisor asked me, "Which of those two workers will accomplish the most today?" The answer seemed obvious. The young fellow with gigantic biceps who could do most anything with ease would certainly beat the older man. Nearing retirement, Charlie moved slowly and appeared to accomplish little. So I made my choice: "The younger worker will accomplish the most work!" The supervisor said, "You're wrong. If you keep watching today, you will notice that the younger worker will take lots of breaks and goof off. The older worker may be slow, but he works at a steady pace all day long." I watched them and, sure enough, Charlie outworked the younger employee.

The strongest person and the super talented may achieve the least. The persistent person and the diligent do accomplish the most. Frankly, failure will certainly result when you refuse to apply yourself with persistence and diligence. The ant may be small, but it has great determination. Take a lesson from the ant!

Journal reflection:

____

____

____

____

____

____

____

____

Marching Through the Poop

Scriptural insight:

Then he said unto me, Lo, I have given thee cow's dung for man's dung, and thou shalt prepare thy bread therewith. (Ezekiel 4:15)

Finding poop Scriptures in the Bible for our daily reading presented a challenge. I'm sure that many who read this will wonder why we included a poop verse and poop devotional in this book. I've also asked myself why God included such a story in His Word. The nation of Israel had rebelled and transgressed against God (Ezekiel 2:3). Ezekiel began to take some strange and interesting actions to draw attention to that fact (Ezekiel 4–5). For instance, God moved upon Ezekiel to use signs to warn Israel of their impending captivity. He would finally mete out judgment upon His wayward people.

In one instance, God instructs Ezekiel to bake some bread with dung, showing the nation of Israel that he would replace the milk and honey of the Promised Land with dung-filled bread. They stood and watched as Ezekiel made the bread. The impact of God's visible sign must have been disturbing. God let them know that they would eat the byproducts of their sin and rebellion.

Devotional focus:

An education major told me about an embarrassing incident that had occurred as her high school marching band performed in a local parade. As she concentrated on playing her instrument and staying even with the musician beside her, she failed to notice that the marchers in front of her had abruptly swerved to avoid something in the road. Her instrument blocked her vision, preventing her from seeing that a horse in front of the band had had a big problem. By the time she realized what had happened, she had no time to avoid the poop and marched right through it. Such funny but humiliating moments you want to keep to yourself.

All students occasionally feel as though they must make their way through pointless situations. Perhaps they feel that a professor has singled them out for embarrassment or has assigned projects or research papers that have little educational value. Usually, however, an instructor sees some potential lying dormant in students. What you consider mistreatment often serves as his attempt to make you a better person. Only much later and in unexpected ways do we see the benefits of many lessons we receive. We may have to deal with misunderstandings in the dorm, or we may end up doing all the work at our part-time job, while other workers get by with doing little.

If you use the word "poop" to refer to being abused, misunderstood, unappreciated, or treated unfairly, then you can expect to march through some poop in this life. Dropping out of the parade means missing out on wonderful opportunities, and this must never be an option. You may sometimes be able to sidestep the poop; other times, you will just endure, marching right through it. By the way, the young lady did survive her ordeal. She still wears a funny smile when she talks about marching in a parade.

Journal reflection:

Beat the Odds

Scriptural insight:

And Jonathan climbed up upon his hands and upon his feet, and his armour-bearer after him: and they fell before Jonathan; and his armour-bearer slew after him: And that first slaughter, which Jonathan and his armour-bearer made, was about twenty men. (1 Samuel 14:13-14)

They call it "trash talk." I refer to what players of opposing teams say to each other before or during a game. Trash talk dates from long ago. Jonathan and his armor bearer heard the Philistines talk trash just before they fought. It went something like this, "Look, the Hebrews have come forth out of the holes where they have been hiding. Come on over here to us, and we will show you something!" (1 Samuel 14:11-12).

Greatly outnumbered, Jonathan and his armor bearer faced the Philistines. Jonathan, however, had great faith that the Lord would strengthen and help them to be victorious. He had earlier said to his armor bearer, "There is no restraint to the Lord to save by many or by few" (1 Samuel 14:6). He acknowledged God's ability to help them beat the odds. In the end, the bodies of the trash talkers looked like trash strewn across about half an acre (1 Samuel 14:14).

Devotional focus:

Our local Comcast cable television station often presents local news and community events for Prince William County, Virginia, and recently aired an awards ceremony for a special group of graduates. Called "Beat the Odds," the program's sponsors included local bar associations and civic groups across the country. Award recipients, such as a student who had been a foster child, had bravely overcome difficult circumstances to graduate from high school. Another recipient, who had broken the law, had a probation officer who helped him to rise above the mistake and beat the odds. Yet another became the first member of his family to graduate from high school and receive a diploma. The Beat the Odds program recognizes kids who have risen above their problems to achieve academic success. They often receive scholarships that help them continue their education.[1]

A university vice president recently said, "About half of our students who begin their education will actually finish school." So the odds of graduating with a degree from that particular school stand at about 50/50. Many, of course, have a good reason for discontinuing their education. Others, however, drop out on a whim, perhaps because they never really took school seriously, or they failed to exercise discipline in studying or going to class.

If difficulties you face tempt you to quit, I encourage you to beat the odds, whether you have little support from home, struggle academically, or suffer disappointment and setbacks. If you will apply yourself and show tenacity and determination, you can beat the odds.

1. Beat the Odds Award Presentation, July 28, 2007, Comcast Studio 3, Manassas, VA

Journal reflection:

The Holding Pattern

Scriptural insight:

And when David enquired of the Lord, he said, Thou shalt not go up; but fetch a compass behind them, and come upon them over against the mulberry trees. (2Samuel 5:23)

God told David to wait. He wanted to attack his enemy, but God directed him to stand by at a location underneath some mulberry trees. David and his men obeyed and patiently stood waiting for a sign to advance. I can almost picture some of the men shifting from foot to foot. Others no doubt held or rubbed their weapons. Some may have questioned the whole process. Waiting probably tried their patience. But standing and waiting proved later to be just the right strategy for winning their battle.

Suddenly, a rustling in the branches and leaves overhead told them they should advance. Militarily, to attack any earlier or any later could have been a great disaster. God knew the precise moment that the enemy would be at the most vulnerable location. Waiting patiently proved to be the strategy that led to an outstanding victory.

Devotional focus:

No one wants to wait, but our spiritual maturation depends upon it. Waiting certainly tries the patience of the motivated and the visionary, as well as those with gifts of leadership. One day, as we prepared to touch down after a routine flight, the pilot told us we would have to wait. I had had to wait for car traffic before, but never for air traffic. Put into a holding pattern, we had to circle for a few minutes. We waited impatiently, wanting to be on the ground. Finally, the pilot announced that we would be landing, and we touched down.

Along with traffic, the doctor's office, auto service department, and grocer's checkout line all have something in common. When we go to these places, we have to wait. One day, I had the oil changed in my car. The attendant told me the job would take about 45 minutes, but it actually took three hours. I sat there wondering about the long wait. On another occasion, I drove to my office and then made some routine stops. That day, I decided to count the traffic lights along my route. They numbered 131, and I had to stop at 27 lights that day. No wonder we get impatient in traffic.

I have been ready to proceed many times, but God has told me to wait. I hated the holding pattern on the plane, but I would have liked even less our pilot taking the initiative to land on his own. When God puts us in a holding pattern, He does so to clear the way for us. He knows the precise time and way to accomplish His divine plan for us. The next time you find yourself circling, trust the pilot and try to enjoy the flight. When your life fails to move as quickly as you'd like, realize that God may have placed you on hold. Trust His wisdom, His timing, and His purposes. You will arrive right on time, according to God's timetable.

Journal reflection:

___

___

___

___

___

___

___

___

___

___

Fitting In Without Fading Out

Scriptural insight:

And Jesus stood still, and commanded him to be called. And they call the blind man, saying unto him, Be of good comfort, rise; he calleth thee. (Mark 10:49)

Fitting into a community can be complicated. One blind man, Bartimaeus, knew the feeling firsthand. His disability had forced him to become self-supporting. The Bible makes no mention of any home, family, or friends he may have had. No one seems to have had much compassion upon him. When he cried out to Jesus for help, we see people telling him to be quiet. As he cried out louder, their plea for his silence became more insistent.

We learn something wonderful about Jesus from this story. Once Jesus heard his voice, the Lord stood still. The Lord asked them to bring Bartimaeus to Him. The Lord valued this precious man. Jesus then healed Bartimaeus, giving him the miracle of sight. The once-blind beggar no longer felt like an outsider or an outcast. The Lord had taken time for him, had shown him mercy, and had given him a wonderful miracle. After the Lord ministered to him, Bartimaeus might have thought, "I guess I do fit in after all." The Lord has a place where you fit in the body of Christ. He will also help you to make a transition and fit into college or university life.

Devotional focus:

Dr. Marshall Craig, preaching at a southern university, geared his message especially to the students in the audience—to the great athletes, handsome young men, and beautiful young ladies. But as Dr. Craig gave the altar call, he noticed something unusual. Far back in the auditorium, he saw a young man crawling toward the front. He turned to the university president and asked about this student, learning that the crippled boy could get around only on his hands and knees. Dr. Craig waited until he drew near the front and walked down to meet him. The young man asked Dr. Craig if God had a place for him. He felt out of place at the university. He knew God had a place for the athletes and the good-looking students on campus, but he wanted to know if God had a place for a wreck like him. Dr. Craig told the young man that God had been waiting for a wreck like him.[1]

We may consider our life a wreck. We may observe popular students who have scores of friends, while we feel lonely and forsaken. God, however, brings you good news. You do fit into the body of Christ, and God will help you fit into college or university life.

1. Charles Welbourn, quoted in *Encyclopedia of 7700 Illustrations* (Chicago, IL: R.R. Donelley and Sons, Inc., 1979), 1214-1215.

Journal reflection:

Chapter Fourteen

Hard Lessons From Our Mistakes

1. *Lessons From an "F"*
2. *Our Top-Ten List*
3. *The Opt-Out Option*
4. *Caffeine and Adrenaline*
5. *Pulling an All-Nighter*
6. *The Balancing Act*
7. *Revision Decision*

Voices and Choices

"My failures have taught me some of the most important lessons of my life."

"My parents motivated me back home. Here, I've had to learn to motivate myself."

"You need to maintain your health. Sleep right, eat right, and remember to exercise."

"I came out of the university with a degree I couldn't use. I couldn't get a job. I'm now taking some pre-law courses in D.C.

I'd tell students to pursue a degree that they enjoy and can use later in life."

Journal Focus

Journal some entries about important lessons you might have learned from your mistakes. What could you do differently to avoid making these mistakes in the future?

Strength Through Prayer

"Father, all of us have failed and made mistakes. Please help us to learn from them. Also help us to forgive ourselves and to learn that those mistakes can teach us many beneficial lessons. Amen."

Lessons From an "F"

Scriptural insight:

For a just man falleth seven times, and riseth up again. (Proverbs 24:16)

Peter said unto him,Though I should die with thee, yet will I not deny thee. Likewise also said all the disciples. (Matthew 26:35)

Peter must have been feeling especially confident about his strength to face difficult situations. When Jesus had told him that he would fail before morning, Peter had confidently asserted that he would never deny the Lord. No way could he fail. I believe he smugly received the words of Jesus with his ears, but his heart refused to believe the possibility. That night after the authorities arrested Jesus, Peter did indeed deny the Lord three times. Then, as they transferred Jesus from one place to another, He and Peter saw each other. The disciple instantly heard a rooster crowing and knew that he had failed. He went out and wept bitterly. His failure no doubt humiliated him, and he hid behind closed doors in fear.

Jesus wants to lift those who have failed and to give them new opportunities for success. After He had arisen, Jesus made a fire and asked Peter three questions about his love for Him. Each time, Peter affirmed that he loved the Lord. God gave Peter another opportunity that day. He had denied the Lord three times at a fire. Now, he embraced the Lord three times at a fire. Within days, Peter preached a powerful sermon and saw thousands saved. Within the next few years, God used him mightily in establishing the early church. His failure proved neither fatal nor final.

Devotional focus:

The teacher spoke for the first time before a class. He finished his lesson, feeling pleased about the knowledge he had shared. Unfortunately, a young lady made a point of criticizing his ability. She waited until just the right moment and said to her friend, "That was the worse lesson I have ever heard!" Moments earlier, the new teacher had felt pretty good about the lecture. Now, stung by the comment, he stood in shock, the harsh words echoing over and over in his mind. At that moment, he could take action in one of two ways. He could let his failure discourage him, or he could learn a valuable lesson from it. So he said, "I will study and become a better teacher."

I know a brilliant teacher, a singer, and a number of students who all quit because of a failure. As we look at the lives of the patriarchs throughout the Bible, we discover that they often failed in one way or another, and so, too, did the disciples who followed Jesus. No matter what position you hold or what task you attempt, you may fall short. Yet, failure might teach us to have mercy on others who fail and to restore them. It might teach us how to succeed the next time. Always remember that you can learn some valuable lessons from an "F."

Journal reflection:

Our Top-Ten List

Scriptural insight:

For a great door and effectual is opened unto me, and there are many adversaries. (1Corinthians 16:9)

Serving the Lord with all humility of mind, and with many tears, and temptations . . . (Acts 20:19)

Many are the afflictions of the righteous: but the Lord delivereth him out of them all. (Psalm 34:19)

You will find the subject matter in the Old Testament and in the New Testament. I'm talking about trials, temptations, and troubles that came against those who sought to accomplish great tasks. Look at the mighty heroes of the Bible, and you will soon see that every one of them faced challenges.

Paul shed many tears as he faced numerous troubles and adversaries. David advised us that the righteous would suffer many afflictions. Being a target for the enemy in spiritual warfare puts us in a difficult position. Knowing that we must endure a variety of tests can be scary. The word "many" underscores the number of the hardships that we will face.

Even so, the Lord has promised to be with us, as we strive to achieve great undertakings. Look again at those Bible heroes, and you will see outstanding victories. They may have been outnumbered, overwhelmed, perplexed, and fearful at times. However, history shows us that God helped them through their difficult circumstances. He will do the same for us today!

Devotional focus:

Students face many barriers on their road to achievements. This top-ten list enumerates obstacles that often lead to failure and provides valuable insight into potential mistakes that you can easily avoid:

10. Poor time management and procrastination: Using your time poorly and putting off study assignments often results in

being ill-prepared and earning sub par grades, even when you have the ability to succeed.

9. Isolating yourself from others and those who want you to be successful: Loneliness often leads to despair, and despair leads to failure.
8. Bringing unresolved issues with you: Past problems could doom your potential success.
7. Rejecting what teachers and others advise: Refusing to follow directions leads to confusion and unfinished tasks.
6. Keeping a haphazard sleep and diet schedule: Sleep deprivation and poor nutrition lead to skipped classes and missed assignments.
5. Maintaining a negative viewpoint: Attitude affects one's outlook and perception.
4. Letting friends influence you negatively: Destructive behavior often ensues.
3. Maintaining a poor work ethic: Failing to apply yourself or live up to your ability can rob you of success.
2. Refusing to be serious about receiving an education: Partying rather than studying becomes the priority.
1. Poor financial management: Accumulating credit card debt can cause financial stress and discouragement.

Journal reflection:

The Opt-Out Option

Scriptural insight:

Looking unto Jesus the author and finisher of our faith; who for the joy that was set before him endured the cross, despising the shame, and is set down at the right hand of the throne of God. For consider him that endured such contradiction of sinners against himself, lest ye be wearied and faint in your minds. (Hebrews 12:2-3)

And let us not be weary in well doing: for in due season we shall reap, if we faint not. (Galatians 6:9)

People often express surprise when they learn that Jesus could have taken a "W." He had the option of withdrawing from the course that His Father had assigned Him. As He was being arrested, He told Peter that the Father stood ready to send 12 legions of angels to rescue Him (Matthew 26:53). Jesus often withdrew from the crowds to rest. Withdrawing from the assignment that His father had given him, however, offered Him no option if He wanted to complete His assignment of reconciling men back to God (Ephesians 2:14-17). So, He endured, and we can focus upon Him as our example when life throws us a curve.

The disciples and the early church suffered intense persecution. Paul had witnessed one of his friends forsaking Christian service (2 Timothy 4:10). Others may have considered the same action. Paul wrote to the churches of Galatia to encourage them, reminding them that they must stay strong in working for the Lord if they would one day reap the rewards of their labors. Withdrawing was not an option, if they were to finish their course (2 Timothy 4:7).

Devotional focus:

The graduate wanted me to share some valuable advice with you. During his schooling, he had evidently taken many incompletes and had withdrawn from several classes. So he said, "Don't choose incompletes or withdrawals as an option." Everyone knows that, occasionally, you must take one of these actions. Sickness, the death of a family member, or some other tragedy may make this option a necessity. In this event, you must later complete work for the class or take it again as soon as possible. This graduate understood these situations. He spoke, instead, of students falling into the habit of taking an "I" or "W" for no good reason. A low grade on a test or paper might make them think they will flunk the course. Instead of working hard, they look for the easy way out. The consequences of staying in bed and rarely attending classes quite often cause many to consider this option.

One student failed a test miserably. She talked about dropping the course, although her major required it. This meant she would have to take it again later. Knowing that successfully completing the course later would remove an "F" from her transcript, she felt better and decided to tough it out. She passed the remaining tests and received a high grade at the end of the semester. She learned that she could get one low grade without failing completely. She learned that if she could just keep going, the situation would often turn around.

Choosing the opt-out option often becomes a pattern for life, such as when a job gets tough or when a marriage hits a snag. So before choosing this option at school, weigh your decision carefully. Refuse to let opting out become a pattern for the way you handle the hard places of life.

Journal reflection:

____

____

____

____

____

____

____

Caffeine and Adrenaline

Scriptural insight:

And the ravens brought him bread and flesh in the morning, and bread and flesh in the evening; and he drank of the brook. (1 Kings 17:6)

And the barrel of meal wasted not, neither did the cruse of oil fail, according to the word of the Lord, which he spake by Elijah. (1 Kings 17:16)

And as he lay and slept under a juniper tree, behold, then an angel touched him, and said unto him, Arise and eat. And he looked, and, behold, there was a cake baken on the coals, and a cruse of water at his head. And he did eat and drink, and laid him down again. And the angel of the Lord came again the second time, and touched him, and said, Arise and eat; because the journey is too great for thee. (1 Kings 19:5-7)

Elijah often faced overwhelming odds and monumental challenges. In his passion to serve the Lord, he often neglected his body. I believe he received more food miracles than anyone else in the Bible, as recorded in 1 Kings 17-19 (excluding the children of Israel receiving manna for 40 years). Elijah witnessed ravens bringing him bread every morning and evening. Pizza delivery services missed by eons being the first to deliver. This miracle occurred because God had ordered the prophet into hiding in a place with no food sources. Another time, Elijah ate the last cake that a desperate mother had baked for herself and her son, and then God miraculously provided them with a continuous supply of meal and oil. Elijah finally collapsed in a state of exhaustion and depression, and he prayed to die. When he awoke, an angel provided food for him and told him that he needed to eat because he had a great journey ahead.

Now, we may never receive a food miracle or see an angel who encourages us to eat. We do know, however, that failing to take nourishment for our bodies will soon cause us to collapse. God cared about an exhausted, depleted, hungry, tired, and depressed prophet, who ate, received strength, and continued to serve God with a great passion.

Devotional focus:

The student thought he could survive on caffeine. He rarely ate, and he ignored those who pointed out that he could not exist on coffee alone. He also depended upon adrenaline to supply the energy necessary to meet the many tasks of school. Suddenly, he fell to pieces. He realized almost too late that he needed more than caffeine and adrenaline to survive and function. This wake-up call prompted him to start taking better care of himself. He began resting more, eating nutritious food, and pacing himself.

We have only one body. To keep it healthy, we must maintain it. We must make sure that we use wisdom with our sleeping and eating habits, study routines, relaxation, and time management. Make sure to allow time in your busy schedule to take care of yourself.

I once had a nice 1957 Chevy, but I let my busy schedule side-track me from checking the oil. Then, one day, much to my surprise, my oil light came on as I drove down the road. The engine started making a lot of noise and quickly died, as I sat on the side of the road thinking how foolish I had been. Avoid becoming so busy that you fail to maintain your body, or you may suddenly find yourself on the side of the road!

Journal reflection:

____

____

____

____

____

____

____

Pulling an All-nighter

Scriptural insight:

I am weary with my groaning; all the night make I my bed to swim; I water my couch with my tears. (Psalms 6:6)

I will both lay me down in peace, and sleep: for thou, Lord, only makest me dwell in safety. (Psalm 4:8)

I laid me down and slept; I awaked; for the Lord sustained me. (Psalm 3:5)

David knew from experience about restless nights, but not because he suffered from insomnia. Rather, his wakefulness evolved from his being a fugitive. David knew that King Saul felt jealous of him, because the people of Israel loved and admired him. So David had to run and hide continually. His sleep left him, because he knew that fearless soldiers sought to kill him, and because he felt cold, hungry, thirsty, tearful, and fearful. He writes in Psalms about his night tears soaking his bed, but Psalms also shows him making a transition. He learned to trust in the Lord. He learned that God would care for him. So he placed his life and future into God's hands and learned to sleep like a baby.

Devotional focus:

Have you ever thought about the forces that rob us of a good night's sleep? Insects buzz and bite. Pets may meow and bark. Rodents may gnaw and scamper. Storms may produce lightening and thunder. Beds may feel too soft or too hard. The temperature may be too warm or too cool. Food and beverages may cause indigestion or contain caffeine. Neighbors may have loud cars or stereos. Roommates may snore or have the sniffles. Pre-test jitters may fill us with anxiety. Deadlines for papers or projects may draw near.

Most people want a good night's sleep. A good night's sleep helps us maintain good health. Adults need between seven and nine hours of sleep a night to function properly. A good night's sleep may benefit you in almost miraculous ways. It reinvigorates you, helping you to discover replenished strength. You feel better physically and mentally. Even your attitude may improve. Everything looks better in the morning, after a good night's sleep. Most college students know they need a good night's sleep, yet they dislike giving in to the urge to go to bed early. Others even make fun of those who do so. I've seen many night owls accidentally sleep through their classes. Night owls walk around like zombies and miss out on a great deal.

You may occasionally need to pull an all-nighter. Perhaps you're in a tight spot because you have a test scheduled the next morning or have a paper due. A demanding schedule has prevented your being prepared. So you bite the bullet and pull an all-nighter. You see students in this position at student centers or all-night restaurants, as they cram for a test, finish a research paper, or prepare for the next day.

Avoid pulling an all-nighter unless you absolutely must. Try to find time to prepare for responsibilities ahead of time. Why not try pulling an all-nighter in bed? You will be surprised at how much it will help you.

Journal reflection:

The Balancing Act

Scriptural insight:

But as for me, I will walk in mine integrity. . . . My foot standeth in an even place. (Psalm 26:11-12)

But as for me, my feet were almost gone; my steps had well nigh slipped. (Psalm 73:2)

A time to weep, and a time to laugh; a time to mourn, and a time to dance. (Ecclesiastes 3:4)

And he said unto them, Come ye yourselves apart into a desert place, and rest a while: for there were many coming and going, and they had no leisure so much as to eat. (Mark 6:31)

A sudden fall can cause embarrassment, injuries, and even death. We often face falls other than physical ones. Falling to pieces emotionally or psychologically or watching someone we love experience such a collapse can cause deep pain. We see Jesus encouraging his disciples to go into a desert place and rest. They had given of themselves in ministry, and they desperately needed to recharge their batteries, just as Jesus did on occasion. He took the disciples to a place of solitude, so they could rest and gain strength to face the new challenges of ministry.

Solomon told us that life consists of both weeping and laughter. He reminded us that life has mourning, and it also has the joy of dancing. This wise man portrayed life as consisting of ups and downs. We must strive to exhibit wisdom as we maintain a healthy balance in our lives.

Devotional focus:

As a child, I watched a circus performer on television attempting to walk from one building to another on a wire more than 100 feet in the air. He chose to perform his act without a net. Unfortunately, a sudden breeze caused the high wire to shake and, though he struggled to maintain his balance, he plunged to his death. His family later said that he had taken many risks in his life. His dangerous choices had led to his great notoriety and success. The family said that they would continue in his tradition.

Some students certainly relate to trying to maintain their equilibrium. Though not on a high wire, they struggle to keep steady. You may struggle to keep your balance as you look at a few of your responsibilities, disciplines and activities. Studying, dating, social interaction, friendships, class meetings, tests, recreation, relaxation, preparing papers and projects, sleeping, working, reading, and eating all have an important place. However, if you lose your balance, a devastating fall may occur.

One student in his junior year had to be rushed to the hospital for a suspected heart attack. Instead, the doctor's report revealed his lack of care for himself. Another student suddenly began to cry uncontrollably, and a nurse revealed that he was on the verge of a breakdown. He had ignored the many warnings from others while pushing himself for long periods of time without sleep and proper nutrition.

As a student, you need the proper food and sleep, and you need to study and be prepared for tests. You must maintain the right balance to be successful. Surviving means hitting the books, but it also means closing them. Too much fun can lead to failure, and no fun at all can lead to failure. Remember to keep your balance!

Journal reflection:

____

____

____

____

____

____

____

Revision Decision

Scriptural insight:

Take fast hold of instruction; let her not go: keep her; for she is thy life. (Proverbs 4:13)

My son, attend to my words; incline thine ear unto my sayings. Let them not depart from thine eyes; keep them in the midst of thine heart. For they are life unto those that find them, and health to all their flesh. Keep thy heart with all diligence; for out of it are the issues of life. (Proverbs 4:20-23)

People listen when public figures talk about important matters. For instance, they carefully scrutinize the words of a president, senator, or congressman, often writing them down for posterity. Many words that dignitaries have shared throughout history have become a part of our cultural heritage. Take these famous quotes from two of our presidents. One called the day the Japanese bombed Pearl Harbor "a day that will live in infamy." One urged Americans to "ask not what your country can do for you—ask what you can do for your country."

When the wisest man in the world speaks, we certainly need to listen. History has given that title to Solomon. As a young man he prayed for wisdom, and God gave him that gift that uniquely qualified him as the wisest man that has ever lived. This man continued to stress the importance of receiving wisdom. He constantly told us that wisdom should be sought and kept securely. He let us know that wisdom would have many wonderful blessings that would touch many areas of our lives.

Whose words do you remember? Is their input constructive or destructive? Are their words negative or positive? Do their words encourage or discourage you? Where will their advice lead you? Do you ever spend time reading the words and receiving the direction of the Bible?

Devotional focus:

Many events and incidents in life cause us to spend countless hours reflecting upon them. Scores of conversations and experiences prompt us to look within to examine ourselves. We all have a tendency to spend too much time thinking about the trivial and too little time thinking about the important issues of life.

You have bravely faced this semester, made many adjustments, survived the trauma of transition, made some new friends, and been exposed to lots of new ideas. The start of a semester brings expectations, while the end of a semester should bring reflection and introspection. It would be a terrible shame to finish a semester without processing the important events that have transpired. Perhaps it is time for a revision decision. How have you grown this semester? Does this growth include intellectual, emotional, and spiritual growth? Have you made mistakes this semester? What can you do to make adjustments that will prevent you from repeating your mistakes? What have you learned this semester about your talents, abilities, gifts, and purpose? What has been your greatest accomplishment this semester?

Now is a good time to reflect, to revise, and, if needed, to redirect some of your time or energy. Reflection and introspection can help you to make some revision decisions that will lead you into even greater success and satisfaction in life.

Journal reflection:

____

____

____

____

____

____

____

Chapter Fifteen

Overcoming Potential Obstacles

1. *The Unknown Graduate*
2. *Your Biggest Tests*
3. *Caught in the Current*
4. *Marks on the Wall*
5. *A New Course*
6. *The Paper Boy*
7. *The Paper Chase*

Voices and Choices

"Talk to older students. They have special insight. They can tell you how to avoid lots of painful experiences."

"The biggest problem that I've seen as a professor is that kids can do the work, but they wait too long to get started. Then they are so stressed that they have trouble finishing it."

"I attended schools all over the place. I didn't have any direction. I later discovered that I had taken lots of classes that I didn't need. Many of them would not transfer. I made a big mistake."

"My roommate would have friends in, and they would stay up late at night. Then, when I had a friend in, my roommate was hostile. I felt like a guest in my own room. Roommates must respect each other."

Journal Focus

What have been the biggest obstacles that you have faced this semester? What have you learned about overcoming them? Journal some thoughts about the lessons you have learned.

Strength Through Prayer

"Heavenly Father, Your Word promises us that You will help us to be overcomers. Please help me experience that promise as I face difficult situations. Amen."

The Unknown Graduate

Scriptural insight:

When my father and my mother forsake me, then the Lord will take me up. (Psalm 27:10)

We will never know what inspired the Psalmist to write about parents who choose to abandon their children. Perhaps he felt abandoned, or maybe he knew the feelings of being forsaken. This same story could well be a headline in one of our papers today. We constantly read stories about parents who mistreat, abuse, and even kill their own children. These stories never fail to shock and sadden us.

God's Word holds a promise for battered, neglected, and forsaken children. Most of us will never know the depth of an abused child's hurt. We may never see the tears they shed as they remember their mistreatment. I'm thankful that they can discover a God Who loves them with an everlasting love. He sees every tear, lifts the wounded, and gives inner healing. A loving Father, He can help hurting victims move beyond the abuse.

Devotional focus:

The class appeared to be just another ordinary session, but the professor's comments made a strong and lasting impression upon me, as he spoke about the upcoming graduation. A young lady about to receive her degree had been a close friend of his for a long time. While he kept her identity confidential, he shared a few details of her past, as a tear formed in his eye. He said, "One of our graduates this year suffered as a victim of abuse. In fact, she and two of her sisters all endured mistreatment at the hands of their father. Even so, she refused to let this exploitation stop her. She has survived it, pulled her life back together, and will walk across the platform and graduate."

Students often leave home to attend school while carrying dark secrets and bearing deep pain. They often feel unwanted and unloved. They feel ill-treated, abandoned, and confused. They wonder if they can ever overcome the shame of their past. The story of this young lady provides encouragement. She moved beyond her abuse to achieve success. She refused to let her past ruin her future. She discovered that her heavenly Father loved her with a pure love that healed, soothed, and restored her dignity. I've never met her nor do I know her identity, but I'm proud that I've heard her story. I'm thankful that the professor shared with us the courage, strength, and success of this graduate.

Journal reflection:

Your Biggest Tests

Scriptural insight:

And Moses said unto the people, Fear not: for God is come to prove you. (Exodus 20:20)

But as for me, I will walk in mine integrity. (Psalm 26:11)

The integrity of the upright shall guide them. (Proverbs 11:3)

We see the reality of God testing His people all through the pages of God's Word. God led Israel into diverse places and brought them face to face with difficult circumstances as He proved (tested) them. While enduring those hard places, they learned lessons of trust and obedience. We also see various patriarchs enduring testing times.

- Abraham walked up a mountain with his son to make a sacrifice (Genesis 22).
- Jacob wrestled with a heavenly warrior (Genesis 32).
- Joseph endured a pit, Potiphar's wife, and prison (Genesis 37-41).
- David experienced the wilderness (Psalm 26:2).
- Shadrach, Meshach, and Abednego passed through a fiery furnace. (Daniel 3)
- Daniel spent the night in a lion's den (Daniel 6).

Testing times, rather than giving God new information about us, teach us some valuable lessons about ourselves and about faithfully trusting and serving God. He does give us pop quizzes, but they always benefit us. Instructors remain silent when giving tests. The silence you often feel during your test is not abnormal.

Devotional focus:

What forms of test do you like best? Some prefer multiple-choice questions, while others prefer fill-in-the-blank, essay, or true-or-false tests. I find it amazing how quickly your pulse can accelerate from normal to rapid once the instructor hands you a test. Many people say, "I'm not a test taker," but, if you have ever passed a test, you are a test taker. Avoid minimizing your potential or ability.

What do you consider the most difficult test you have ever taken? Why? Did you dislike the subject? Perhaps you found it too long and complex. We seem to remember the hardest tests that we have faced with unpleasant and uneasy feelings. It may shock you to learn that the hardest tests of life will occur outside of a classroom and without a professor to administer them. You will find them more personal and much more significant. You may even be unaware that you have taken them. Let's look at some of the hardest tests of life while you ask yourself some vital questions.

- Will I live a life of integrity?
- Will I have patience to endure God's molding process?
- Will I practice self-control?
- Will I respect authority even when I disagree?
- Will I apply myself to the best of my ability?

These tests come not as midterms or finals lasting a couple of hours, rather they occur throughout your life. A passing grade will determine what you truly become.

Journal reflection:

____

____

____

____

____

____

____

____

Caught in the Current

Scriptural insight:

. . . all thy waves and thy billows are gone over me. (Psalm 42:7)

Then the waters had overwhelmed us, the stream had gone over our soul: Then the proud waters had gone over our soul. (Psalm 124:4-5)

King David experienced major highs and lows in his life. Anointed at an early age, he had both success and strength. Yet, as a young adult, he felt desperate, fearful, and hopeless. Many of the songs from Psalms express the terrible emotions that swept over him as he wrote and sang his tearful songs. One would think that facing Goliath would have inspired some feelings of fear that would have inspired a song. Yet, he faced this giant without intimidation, fear, or, seemingly, even dread. He stood with confidence, assured of victory.

Running from King Saul's elite soldiers had a far greater impact upon David. While the encounter with Goliath lasted minutes, he spent several years as a fugitive. During many close calls, David's life must have flashed before his eyes. His writings portray the candid and raw emotions of a man who feels overwhelmed. He tells of running, hiding, being lonely, feeling abandoned, and questioning God's will as well as experiencing hopelessness and disappointment. David's experiences should encourage anyone who feels the pain and tears that life often brings. If fear and sadness overtake you, try reading the Psalms.

David survived his horrific experience. History lets us know that he made his way through the years of pain and struggle. The waves and billows that overflowed his life did not drown him. He finally achieved his destiny and enjoyed a life of success as Israel's second king.

Devotional focus:

I saw my family staring at me. Then, my father cautioned me to move away from the shoals in the river, a series of small waterfalls that extended about 200 feet and dropped about 50 feet. I guess I enjoyed the attention, or maybe I wanted to show off. Already in the middle of the river, I inched a little closer to the edge of the falls. My family looked anxious, and I laughed. Suddenly, I felt the current moving much stronger than I had imagined. I had gotten too close to the edge, too far to turn around. The current swept me down the river. I still remember tumbling over and over, out of control. My left leg smashed into a huge rock and began to turn numb. Several times, I sank way down into some deep pools of water and slowly resurfaced, only to be swept over more rocks. I arrived at the bottom of the falls barely able to walk. I realized how stupid I had been and how fortunate I was to come out alive.

That incident serves as a good illustration of what can happen to students. Rather than the current of river waterfalls, students should worry about being caught in the current of other dangerous activities. As we have interviewed students, their comments warning about harmful practices that occur on most campuses have astounded us. Consider drinking, drugs, and sex like the current of a river. These activities bring excitement, but students caught in their power will find themselves tumbling out of control. They find themselves incapable of breaking free. Sorrowfully, we all know of individuals who have lost their lives, become hopelessly addicted, or contracted an STD.

Realize that getting too close to dangerous situations can be harmful. Avoid getting caught up in such behavior. Refuse to let the peer pressure of those who like to party persuade you to act foolishly. Don't get caught in the current!

Journal reflection:

____

____

____

____

Marks on the Wall

Scriptural insight:

Till we all come in the unity of the faith, and of the knowledge of the Son of God, unto a perfect man, unto the measure of the stature of the fullness of Christ. (Ephesians 4:13)

Paul told the disciples at the Ephesus church that they should desire spiritual growth and the fullness of Christ (Ephesians 4:13-14). He said we should measure our spiritual maturity by how much we resemble Jesus Christ. Paul challenged the body of Christ to pursue spiritual growth and anticipated spiritual maturity in the lives of these believers.

We experience spiritual, physical, and mental growth, all of which takes time. Just as men and women take years to mature physically, they also may mature slowly in other areas. Students face the challenge of growing mentally. Mental growth is evidenced through maturity, wisdom, and knowledge. While the physical body usually grows naturally, our minds need the challenges that come through professors, research papers, projects, and tests. Mental growth takes a lot of hard work, time, and discipline.

Devotional focus:

Children, at a certain point in their lives, often become concerned about growth. Some kids have a parent or friend monitor their growth with marks on a wall or notches on a doorframe. They stand and stretch as a new mark or notch shows their growth. They turn around with great expectation and stare at the mark or notch. Sometimes, they complain that they see no change. I remember going through the same ritual with my mother when I was about 10 years old. I wondered if I would ever grow up.

Like a child who eagerly looks at the marks, we wish we could see some sign of growth. Students rarely seem to see themselves growing as they routinely attend classes, take tests, and finish projects. The daily grind of school often makes students despair of getting anywhere. Perhaps your growth (the mark or notch) will be apparent as you talk to others. They see significant changes in your life, even though you seem oblivious to them. I've talked with freshmen as they began their educational journey, and I've talked with them after they graduated. They seem unaware of the great changes that I see in them—their growth in ability, confidence, and maturity.

Growing up, I would attend family gatherings, and I would be surprised when an aunt or uncle would say, "My, how you have grown!" I neither felt nor saw change in myself, but they saw it. Just so, those around you see your growth, and they see your development and maturity when they say, "My, how you have grown!"

Journal reflection:

A New Course

Scriptural insight:

Who hath delivered us from the power of darkness, and hath translated us into the kingdom of his dear Son. (Colossians 1:13)

Kid's Konnection, a powerful ministry to children in Washington, D.C., often provides food, clothing, toys, and spiritual guidance. The group tells children Bible stories on sidewalks, in parks, and elsewhere. This charitable organization's work demonstrates the power of the Bible to transform lives, changing and blessing thousands on these violent streets, so that many of the kids choose a new course for their future. Kid's Konnection has a children's choir that travels to local churches around Washington. The singers visited my church one Sunday morning, and I'll never forget one 12-year-old boy's testimony. He grew up on the streets, hanging around the wrong kind of people, a product of his environment. He told how the Lord had changed his life. "I was going to be a hit man," he confessed. Before he came to Jesus Christ, he intended to become a professional killer. The gospel of Jesus Christ had transformed him. Several years later, I asked about this young man and learned that he thrives in school, preparing for a different kind of mission in life. Instead of taking lives, he now works to rescue them. The big change in this young man reminds me that the gospel really does change people—and events.[1] Paul let us know that the gospel can make radical changes in lives.

Devotional focus:

A would-be hit man accepted transformation, his life greatly altered. Many events cause us to modify our route, often for the better, but many times for the worse. Some adjustments come instantly; but others, gradually. Let's look at some influences that change lives:

- Peer pressure. Some will carry out terrible acts of violence and immorality on a friend's advice. I've seen these acts result in loss of life or a lifetime of pain. Others, influenced in a different way, attempt and accomplish great works, thanks to a friend's influence. Are your friendships changing you into a better person?

- Family influence. Our home situation and upbringing impact all of us. Often the family environment harms children and influences them negatively. Kids often grow to adulthood feeling worthless after a life of verbal abuse. Other kids, through positive feedback, have built self-esteem. Do you know that people can rise above negative family influence? Ask the young man from Kid's Konnection.
- Salvation. Paul called himself the chief of sinners. Others tell similar stories, revealing that God's love, mercy, and forgiveness do transform people. Have you allowed the gift of salvation to change you?
- Education. One of the greatest influences to change, a good education teaches students to think. It opens doors of opportunity and gives career choices. Do you recognize what a good education can do for you?

Many pressures exist in the world today. Have you examined the influences in your life that push you to modify your path? Do you know that you can rise above negative influences? Are the changes in your life making you a better person?

[1] Used by permission of The Kid's Konnection Children's Ministry of Washington, D.C.

Journal reflection:

____

____

____

____

The Paper Boy

Scriptural insight:

And when they came to Marah, they could not drink of the waters of Marah, for they were bitter: therefore the name of it was called Marah. And the people murmured against Moses, saying, What shall we drink? And he cried unto the Lord; and the Lord shewed him a tree, which when he had cast into the waters, the waters were made sweet. (Exodus 15:23-25)

Long before God delivered Israel from Egypt, He had placed a small tree near a bitter stream. The tree grew while the children of Israel served as slaves making bricks. The tree grew while God poured out the locusts, lice, frogs, and other pestilences upon Egypt. The tree grew as Israel walked upon dry ground in the midst of the Red Sea. Finally, a thirsty nation arrived at the stream. Those who drank first complained of the water's bitter taste. God instructed Moses to cut down the tree and cast it into the water. Then, the water became sweet to drink. Long before Israel arrived, God had planted and prepared this tree. He had planned and instituted a solution before they ever faced the problem.

Facing difficult decisions—the bitter waters of life—often leaves us confused about a course of action. We can take comfort in knowing that God already knows what we will face and goes ahead to prepare the way. He knew beforehand which school we would choose, and He knows about the greatest struggles we must endure. He has a solution for our problems even before we get to them. God knows what our future holds!

Devotional focus:

A paperboy named Charles stood on a street corner in Danville, Virginia. He felt God's call upon his life, and he dreamed about attending school to become a minister. His family had limited finances, so attending any school would take a miracle. As he stood there, Charles told a friend about his calling and his dream, unaware that God had already been working in his future. At that precise moment, a pastor walked by, and the paperboy's friend called him over, telling him about the paperboy's situation. The minister promised to help Charles, who soon had the promise of a four-year scholarship, and he did attend college.[1] As a student, however, he made poor grades, much lower than he had anticipated. He brought his report card home to his mother with lots of "Ds" in evidence, and she asked him a question: "Is that the best you can do?" When he answered, "Yes," she said, "Let's pray about it." He remembers those days fondly, noting that, "She never criticized, compared, or condemned me."[2] Today, Dr. Charles Stanley pastors a large church in Atlanta. He still testifies that God gave him a miracle, and that God works to help us achieve our purposes in life.

1. Dr. Charles Stanley, In Touch Ministries, March 26, 2006.
2. Dr. Charles Stanley, In Touch Ministries, June 24, 2007.

Journal reflection:

The Paper Chase

Scriptural insight:

And, The labourer is worthy of his reward. (1 Timothy 5:18)
In all labour there is profit. (Proverbs 14:23)

People who lived in Biblical times knew about hard work. They had to draw water and carry it to their homes. Many had fields to plow, plant, harvest, and maintain, as well as vines and fruit trees to preserve and to harvest. They had flocks and herds to tend and protect. Families reaped the benefits of their labor through the food they ate and the income their work generated. The people of Biblical times, however, really had no choice in performing some of these tasks. They had to get up early and work hard to survive.

Today, we have the option of pursuing various career choices and job opportunities. When we submit our resume and application, we hope that the employer will contact us. When he does, we find it exciting to hear that we have the job. The initial meeting with a company's personnel department usually requires us to submit our Social Security number, claim our dependants, and learn about any training program and expectations. The employer will talk about salary structure and discuss the method of payment. Perhaps we will choose to have our check deposited into a bank account or given straight to us. The personnel staff will inform us of extras that go with the job, including insurance for our family, profit sharing, vacation and sick leave, yearly bonuses, and retirement benefits.

As a student, you receive no pay to attend classes. Rather, you must pay to go to school. At the end of pursuing an education, however, your schooling will open doors and give you benefits that you may never have expected. The Bible reminds us of the reward and profit in labor.

Devotional focus:

When you enrolled in college, you began a journey toward a degree. A printed piece of paper that weighs barely an eighth of an ounce, most diplomas measure about 10 inches wide by 8 inches tall. The degree will state the name of the institution and the location of your school. Your degree may declare something like, "The Board of Directors of [school's name] upon the recommendation of the faculty and by virtue of the authority vested in them have conferred on [your name], who has satisfactorily completed the studies and fulfilled all the requirements thereof the degree of [name of degree you have received], And is entitled to the rights, privileges and honors pertaining to that degree and has been granted this diploma on the [date of your graduation]." Several names will appear at the bottom of the degree. Once you receive it, you will probably have it framed, placing it in an office or hanging it in a special location at home for others to see.

At first, you will stare at it a lot and show your degree to others. Within a few years, you will rarely look at it. It may even collect some dust. You will only think about your degree when someone asks you the name of your school and major. The real power of your degree lies in the doors it opens and the opportunities it gives you. Like a benefits package, it entitles you to many rights and privileges. Your paper chase may often be difficult, but your labor will eventually crown your life with many wonderful benefits and rewards.

Journal reflection:

____

____

____

____

____

____

____

____

Chapter Sixteen

Final Reflections and Thoughts

1. *It's Worth It All*
2. *Regrets and Accomplishments*
3. *Tassels and Tears*
4. *If I Had It To Do Over Again*
5. *One Final Lesson*
6. *Something Worth Remembering*
7. *Our Prayer for You*

Voices and Choices

"College was very positive for me. It gave me a good foundation to enter the military. This served as the foundation for my military training. Following the military, my education opened up some wonderful doors for my career."

"My advice is to finish college while you are there. It is hard to go back."

"That's where I messed up. I didn't keep going."

"Attending a university and receiving my degree has opened up a lot of doors for me in life."

"Dedicate yourself to getting everything you can get while you are at school."

Journal Focus

Journal some of the feelings you are experiencing as this semester ends. Also, journal some thoughts as you look ahead toward your future graduation. Write some final memories in your journal that you can read in years to come.

Strength Through Prayer

"Dear Lord, thank You for giving me strength to finish this semester. Thank You for new friends and the lessons I have learned. I pray that You will lead, guide, and direct me as I face the challenges that lie ahead. Amen."

It's Worth It All

Scriptural insight:

For I reckon that the sufferings of this present time are not worthy to be compared with the glory which shall be revealed in us. (Romans 8:18)

We make comparisons about products, places, and people all the time. A recent conversation revealed that an individual preferred one pain reliever over another. A different conversation showed that one person favored a particular automobile, while another preferred a different one. Two people recently disagreed about which restaurant ranked the highest. I've also heard individuals compare churches, saying that one has a better youth program, while another has better music. Some people prefer to hear one pastor; others like a pastor down the road. We will always make comparisons.

In writing to a church enduring great persecution, Paul used comparisons to help the disciples. He wanted to comfort them, helping them to put their situation in the right perspective. He told them how unworthy their momentary sufferings and hardships appeared in comparison to the eternal glory that awaited them. Weeks, months, or years of persecution, even the agony of martyrdom, pales when compared to eternal peace and rest. Living without life's material blessings fails in comparison to an eternal inheritance (1 Peter 1:4), including the heavenly home that awaits us (John 14:2-3). I believe the church got his point. History records their faithfulness, and they soon discovered for themselves that their inheritance ranked beyond compare.

Devotional focus:

As you headed off to college, someone likely asked you how much you would be paying for your education. If you had done your research, you would have been able to give them a ballpark figure. Then, their second question was probably, "Do you think it will be worth all that money?" We have all heard comparisons about how much more money a graduate as opposed to a non-graduate earns during a lifetime, but you can ascertain the worth of your degree only if you use the education you've gained.

Graduates will tell you that receiving a degree makes the money and effort worth it. You may have to commute many miles, buying a lot of gas, but it's worth it all! You will spend hours studying and preparing papers. You will lose sleep and often feel exhausted. You will lose contact with some friends and miss your family. You may live for a time in a cramped dorm with some vastly different people. You may even have to repay some student loans. In the face of all these hardships, however, it is worth it all!

Journal reflection:

Regrets and Accomplishments

Scriptural insight:

And when he came to himself, he said, How many hired servants of my father's have bread enough and to spare, and I perish with hunger! I will arise and go to my father, and will say unto him, Father, I have sinned against heaven, and before thee. . . . But the father said to his servants, Bring forth the best robe, and put it on him; and put a ring on his hand, and shoes on his feet. (Luke 15:17-18, 22)

The story of the prodigal son, one of the most powerful stories in the Bible, shows a beautiful picture of the Gentiles coming to God. The father represents God, the elder brother represents Israel, and the younger son represents the Gentiles. This story also illustrates the great mercy and grace of God, who forgave us, accepted us, and made us part of His family.

This powerful narrative speaks to the prodigals of today. God has the power to forgive them, and He welcomes them back home. I want you to notice that the father never talked about his son's mistakes. He never chided him for wasting money. He simply loved, forgave, restored, and embraced his son. God offers those who come to Him a new beginning.

Devotional focus:

The words of a young man of about the age of 23 at a fast-food restaurant startled me. I had told him that our kids' moving into the local university had brought us to town. Then, as he filled my order for a sausage biscuit and coffee, he said, "That's where I messed up. I didn't go on and continue my education!" He spoke with such total despair that it stunned me into silence. I hardly expected him to tell me about his mistake, his regrets, and his lost opportunity. I wondered why he had given up on his dream, what events had caused him to quit, what kept him from going back to finish his education. Other customers waiting prevented my talking further with him.

The speaker let everyone know her age, proud to be 64 and graduating from the university. Her life had been consumed with parental responsibilities as a mother. Now a grandmother, she had obviously hidden her desire deep within her heart. At age 64, her degree would generate few, if any, career opportunities, but it fulfilled her dream. She had returned to the university, finished her degree, and graduated. Today, her memory inspires me.

As I thought about these two individuals and their contrasting attitudes, I realized that one had given up on his goal at age 23, while the other still dreamed at age 64. How I wish I could have told the young man about the grandmother's story.

What I'm going to say may seem trite, but it is, nonetheless, true. Never give up on your dream. Never throw in the towel, no matter how hard it gets. If you have given up, take inspiration from a 64-year-old grandmother who fulfilled her dream. God can still give you strength to complete unfinished business.

Journal reflection:

Tassels and Tears

Scriptural insight:

Get wisdom, get understanding: forget it not; neither decline from the words of my mouth. Forsake her not, and she shall preserve thee: love her, and she shall keep thee. Wisdom is the principal thing; therefore get wisdom: and with all thy getting get understanding. Exalt her, and she shall promote thee: she shall bring thee honour, when thou dost embrace her. She shall give to thine head an ornament of grace: a crown of glory shall she deliver to thee. (Proverbs 4:5-9)

Solomon had experienced bereavement at his father David's death. He would sit on the throne as Israel's new king, a successor to David. From the beginning of his reign, Solomon realized that he would need divine help and, as one of his first acts, offered sacrifices unto the Lord (2 Chronicles 1:6; 2 Chronicles 7:5). The Lord appeared unto Solomon at night and spoke to him, saying, "Ask what I shall give thee" (2 Chronicles 1:7). Solomon longed to be a good king and knew that such a ruler would need wisdom and knowledge to be successful. So Solomon asked God for these two gifts. Not only did God grant his request, but He also gave him wealth and honor.

Solomon's wisdom amazed his subjects and the whole world. For example, in 1 Kings 3:16-28, two women appeared before him, both claiming to be the mother of a live baby, but one mother had accidentally smothered her baby in the night. Solomon called for a sword to divide the remaining child, but the real mother immediately offered to give her child to the other woman to preserve it. Solomon delivered the baby to the real mother.

Throughout the book of Proverbs, Solomon wrote that we should pursue wisdom and understanding, because they will preserve, promote, bring honor, and crown our heads with success.

Devotional focus:

A cap with a tassel may be the nearest most of us will come in this life to wearing a symbol that compares to a crown. I still have mine from my high school graduation. How proud we felt when we donned our cap and stood at the mirror admiring the way we looked. Others must have liked the way we looked, too, because they wanted our graduation pictures. I had great pride at my high school graduation, but shed no tears.

My university graduation affected me differently. My tears ran down as I thought about how often I had wanted to quit and what I had endured. Despite financial difficulties, being overwhelmed, working outside my comfort zone, and struggling academically, I had stayed the course. So tears of joy flowed at my sense of accomplishment, as well as at my realization that the Lord had made my graduation possible. I recognized that He had given me strength, financial help, friends, and everything else it took to lead me to success.

For graduation, seniors have their heads measured and receive their regalia. They proudly wear their cap along with a tassel. For life, the Lord will adorn a graduate's head with the glory of an invisible crown of wisdom and understanding. I hope you feel thankful for your victories that will crown you with a cap, tassel, and the magnificence of being adorned with wisdom and understanding.

Journal reflection:

If I had It To Do Over Again

Scriptural insight:

And they set the ark of God upon a new cart, and brought it out of the house of Abinadab that was in Gibeah. (2 Samuel 6:3)

And the anger of the Lord was kindled against Uzzah; and God smote him there for his error; and he died by the ark of God. (2 Samuel 6:7)

So David went and brought up the ark of God from the house of Obededom into the city of David with gladness. (2 Samuel 6:12)

You feel terrible when you look back and realize that you have made major mistakes. You consider yourself fortunate when you can learn from your blunders. You experience great joy when you can repair missteps in your past.

David had a great desire to bring the ark of God to Jerusalem. He rushed to bring up the ark of God without understanding that God had prescribed a correct way to transport it. A man named Uzzah reached out to stabilize the ark when it appeared to be falling from the cart. He immediately lost his life. I wonder if God wanted us to know that He stabilizes us, and we never have to protect or stabilize Him. Israel then placed the ark in Obededom's home while David reflected on the tragedy.

So David mourned, reflected, asked some questions, and waited. He learned that God had prescribed in detail how the ark should be transported. God afforded him the opportunity to go back and do it over, allowing him to change his methods and transport it God's way. His second attempt proved to be a blessing, both for David and for Israel.

Devotional focus:

The topic of conversation: Do overs. I asked two groups of university graduates the following questions. First, "If you could go back to school and do it again, what would you do differently?" Second, "If you could offer advice to someone just starting his education, what would you tell him?" These graduates offered valuable advice, which, if heeded, could keep new students from making some mistakes and could lead to greater happiness and satisfaction in school. Listen to these words of wisdom from those who have walked your path, as they reflect upon their journey:

"I would have gotten involved sooner. I was too passive."

"Connect early with a local church. It's okay to shop for a church where you feel comfortable. When you find your church, stay there and get involved."

"Don't rush romance."

"Get involved in campus life. Be involved in sports and mixers the school offers. Get your nose out of the book for a while."

"I wish I had chosen a different degree. I would be better equipped."

"Don't choose "I" (Incomplete) as an option unless you absolutely have to."

"Make more friends. Take the time to talk to the people around you."

"Don't isolate yourself from others."

"I would call home more often."

"Make sure that you remain grounded. You must be grounded or you will be swallowed up."

"Too many students at my university gave too much attention to other things. You must focus on why you went to school."

These graduates offered this advice to help you avoid mistakes and to help you make some needed changes and decisions. Why not ask some graduates what they would do differently if they could do it again? I promise that this will be a beneficial and profitable experience.

Journal reflection:

____

____

____

One Final Lesson

Scriptural insight:

Finally, my brethren, be strong in the Lord, and in the power of his might. (Ephesians 6:10)

Finally, brethren, farewell, Be perfect, be of good comfort, be of one mind, live in peace; and the God of love and peace shall be with you. (2 Corinthians 13:11)

Final words often stand as the most important words that we share with others. Paul addressed various churches, dealing with their problems, encouraging them, giving them instructions, and offering prayers for them. As he closed some of his letters, he often shared significant views, such as how much he loved and appreciated his brothers and sisters in the Lord. He often gave personal messages to individuals he wanted to encourage. He occasionally gave a benediction of blessing to strengthen others. Some of his pages probably bore tearstains, as he shared his closing thoughts with those he loved.

We have final thoughts for you that are similar in nature. We celebrate your accomplishments and feel confident that God will give you a wonderful future. We hope and pray that this devotional book has helped you in some way. We have sought to be a blessing to you, and we believe that you will be a blessing to others. We also close our book with great sentiment and tears for each of you.

Devotional focus:

Every student has a first exam as a freshman. Every student has a last exam every semester and a final exam as a senior. That's when the graduating senior may boldly declare, "I've taken my last test as a college student!" The baccalaureate degree will then be awarded, the tassel will be moved, and the cap thrown into the air. You may still, however, need to learn one final lesson.

A few weeks ago I heard an interview on a radio station. I've forgotten the source of the report, however, the reporter interviewed an educator who helped to place college students into the work force. She noted that graduates usually send out resumes without doing any follow-up. Placement studies have revealed that many graduates fail actively to pursue a career.

So we have a final lesson that you may need following your future graduation. You must be proactive in seeking your job or career. Once you have sent your resumes, call and let the company offering the job know of your genuine interest in the position. If appropriate, make an appointment. Be persistent and proactive about putting yourself out there. Try to make as many connections as possible with those in the hiring process. Do your best to make yourself available, and let them know what a great asset you would be for them. Finally, we pray for your future placement, success, and happiness, and we celebrate your future commencement.

Journal reflection:

Something Worth Remembering

Scriptural insight:

These things saith he that is holy, he that is true, he that hath the key of David, he that openeth, and no man shutteth; and shutteth and no man openeth. (Revelation 3:7)

I am shut up, and I cannot come forth. (Psalm 88:8)

Students of theology often use the word "providence." This word has to do with the plans, provisions, and purposes of God regarding the future. Especially relative for every student at the end of college life and facing concerns about the future, this word points to God as the leader, guide, and director in our lives.

The way God works often baffles Christians. Many times, we recognize His handiwork; yet, at other times, we find His ways a mystery. We seldom recognize that He chooses to use different methods to achieve His glory and purposes. Take a look at the following examples:

- God opened up the Red Sea and let Israel cross on dry ground (Exodus 14:22). God led Israel into the Jordan River, and the water slowly receded (Joshua 3:13).
- Jesus spoke the words and healed a blind man (Luke 18:41-43). He also spat and made clay to anoint and heal the eyes of another blind man (John 9:6-7).
- God sent an angel to deliver Peter from prison (Acts 12:7), and He sent an earthquake to do the same for Paul and Silas (Acts 16:26). An engineer once told me that the magnitude of that earthquake showed as big a miracle as the earthquake itself, because its power opened the doors without collapsing the prison.
- Sometimes God opens a door (2 Corinthians 2:12); sometimes God closes a door (Acts 16:6).
- Sometimes God answers instantly (1 Kings 18:38), and sometimes we wait in silence for His answer to our prayers (Psalm 28:1). At other times, He simply says "no" (2 Corinthians 12:9).

Learning to trust in the providence of God always serves our best interests, although it may seem otherwise. Years may pass before we realize how events actually worked out for the best. To learn a lot about how God will work in our lives, we have but to look back at how events have transpired in our past.

Devotional focus:

At some point, every student will struggle to learn the will of God. At times, you may feel crushed that events failed to work out the way you wanted. Sometimes, you may want to go, while He wants you to stay. Or you may want to stay, when He wants you to go. Take a look at these examples of God's providence, will, and perfect timing:

- The graduate received an offer for a position that seemed perfect for him. When he prayed, however, he had a bad feeling about taking the job. He called and declined. Much later he realized that the position would have been one of the worst moves he could have made for his life.
- The student applied for a position that he really wanted, but received no consideration for it. Disappointed at the moment, he later realized what a disaster he would have been in the job, because of his inexperience.
- The student had many roadblocks, arriving at school much later than most students, but the timing turned out to be perfect for the many open doors that followed.
- The student, thrown into a position way over his head, felt overwhelmed, but he learned many valuable lessons about organization and leadership.
- The graduate sought a promotion with another organization. She was certain she would get the position. She was passed over, she felt let down, but she moved on. Two years later, when the organization experienced a big shake-up, she felt she had been protected from great pain and anguish. She later received the same type of position where she was already working.

An open door, a promotion, or an opportunity may be less than optimal for you, and a closed door may eventually prove to be the best occurrence for your life. If you miss out on a promotion, just tell God about your frustration and move forward. We must simply learn to trust God, accept His will, and believe that He works everything out for good in our lives (Romans 8:28).

Journal reflection:

Our Prayer for You

Scriptural insight:

I thank my God upon every remembrance of you, Always in every prayer of mine for you all making request with joy, For your fellowship in the gospel from the first day until now; Being confident of this very thing, that he which hath begun a good work in you will perform it until the day of Jesus Christ. (Philippians 1:3-6)

Paul, a man of prayer, realized the potential for prayer to change circumstances around him. He often wrote many of his prayers in his letters. We gain a great blessing in reading them. He told the church at Philippi that he had been praying for them, letting them know that he had confidence that God would help them complete the work they had begun.

A look at some of the 650 prayers of the Bible reveal that many wonderful changes have occurred after people sought God. He has provided strength, resources, healing, mighty victories, and miracles through prayer. Prayer really does change things.

The student prepared to get married, working several part-time jobs while he finished his final semester. He needed $1,200 to move himself and his new wife into an apartment. After saving every cent he could, he discovered that he had only $600. He feverishly and earnestly prayed for the other $600. Then, one night, a voice awakened a distant relative and kept telling her, "_________ needs your help!" The relative called and asked him to stop by to see her and her husband. When he did, they handed him an envelope containing exactly $600. To his amazement, God had answered his prayer. Remember, prayer really does change things. Also remember that, when you put off praying, you risk potential failure and collapse (Luke 18:1).

Devotional focus:

As we conclude this book, we want to pray a blessing upon your life. We hope that these devotionals have helped you. We wish we could meet and talk with you. We would love to hear about your journey and the dreams that you have within your heart. While meeting everyone who reads this book is impossible, we can offer a prayer on your behalf. Please insert your name into the blanks provided below.

> "Heavenly Father, it has been a great joy for us to write this devotional book. Please let it give valuable instruction and encouragement. First, we ask that you help __________ to survive the challenge of transition. We know that __________ comes to this place with some fears and hurts. Remind __________ that you have the power to comfort and heal. Let __________ know that you always stand ready to help. Second, we ask that you meet __________'s needs. When he/she needs friends, please send them. When finances fall short, please provide them. When he/she feels weak, please supply strength. Give __________ the ability to endure challenges and to overcome disappointments. Make this time valuable, enjoyable, and memorable. Finally, please help __________ to discover his/her gifts and purpose. We ask you to open the doors that you would have __________ to enter. Please make __________ a great success in life. Please prepare __________ for the ultimate test of standing before you when life is over. Amen."

Journal reflection:

Appendix 1

Alphabetical Listing of Devotional Titles

Trivial Pursuit
Two Thousand Six Hundred Eighty-Eight Hours
Unfinished Business
Unpacking All Your Baggage
Utilizing Campus Resources
What Are You Afraid Of?
What Are You Looking At?
What Do You Need to Succeed?
What Is Right With Your School?
When the Melting Pot Boils
When Your Suitemate Is Not Sweet
You Better Recognize
Your Biggest Tests
Your Father Knows
Your Future Starts Now
Your Hidden Strength

Appendix 2

Devotional Topics

Campus Voices and Student Choices is filled with more than 150 quotes from students and graduates, scriptural and devotional lessons, and a student journal. This book is a basic discipleship book written from a Christian perspective to give spiritual insight for the collegiate journey. It offers practical and relevant advice that is sure to help every college student.

The cost of a college degree is staggering. The price of most textbooks is surprising. Nevertheless, tuition payments and the purchase of textbooks are unavoidable. Parents want their children to succeed, so they often help their children prepare for school, purchasing clothes, shoes, personal items, food, bedding, and appliances. Sometimes, they provide financial support as students enroll in the school they have chosen. This new and exciting step will be filled with many challenges and hazards. Every student will need strength and encouragement. That is why ***Campus Voices and Student Choices*** is indispensable.

Why not help students succeed by giving them a resource to assist them with their transition and trauma? This book deals with many issues that students will face, and it provides valuable devotionals that will strengthen, encourage, and help every student to be successful.

Devotional Topics:

Absolutes	Confidence	Friendship	Prayer
Abuse	Conflict	Future	Pressure
Adjustments	Counsel	Gift Discovery	Priorities
Appreciation	Courage	Goals	Problems
Apprehension	Danger	Gratification	Procrastination
Applying Yourself	Decisions	Guidance	Purpose
Attitudes	Depression	Happiness	Questions
Authority	Destiny	Homesickness	Resilience
Baggage	Discipleship	Instructions	Rest
Balance	Discipline	Integrity	Romance
Becoming Marketable	Disappointments	Involvement	Rules
Beginnings	Distractions	Isolation	Salvation
Behavior	Diversity	Loneliness	Sleep
Being Teachable	Dreams	Miracles	Standards
Bible	Endurance	Morality	Stress
Boundaries	Excellence	Motivation	Success
Careers	Expectations	Nutrition	Talents
Challenges	Failure	Opportunities	Tears
Change	Fear	Pain	Temptation
Classroom Success	Finances	Patience	Time
Community	Finishing	Plans	Transformation
Conduct	Fitting In	Potential	Transition

Breinigsville, PA USA
23 December 2009

229655BV00001BA/2/P

9 781607 916802